OUT OF THE NIGHT

To: Maureen
Hope you enjoy the book,
Best Wishes
Marion Warren
x

© Marion Warren, 2019

All rights reserved. Without limiting the rights under copyright reserved above, no part of this publication may be reproduced, stored in or introduced into a retrieval system, or transmitted, in any form or by any means (electronic, mechanical, photocopying, recording or otherwise), without the prior written permission of both the copyright owner and the publisher of this book.

Set in 12/15pt Bembo

Edited by Marion Warren and Bill Scolding

First published in 2019 by
Serpentine Design
3 Coastguard Houses, Cadgwith
Helston, Cornwall TR12 7JZ

www.serpentine-design.com

ISBN: 978-0-9572851-2-5

OUT OF THE NIGHT

*The experiences of a World War II
bomber pilot and prisoner-of-war*

BILL WARREN

INVICTUS

Out of the night that covers me,
 Black as the pit from pole to pole,
I thank whatever gods may be
 For my unconquerable soul.

In the fell clutch of circumstance
 I have not winced nor cried aloud.
Under the bludgeonings of chance
 My head is bloody, but unbowed.

Beyond this place of wrath and tears
 Looms but the Horror of the shade,
And yet the menace of the years
 Finds and shall find me unafraid.

It matters not how strait the gate,
 How charged with punishments the scroll,
I am the master of my fate,
 I am the captain of my soul.

William Ernest Henley, 1849 - 1903

CONTENTS

Chapter 1	A Kingsbridge Childhood, 1920 – 1937	9
Chapter 2	Airman, Second Class, 1938	38
Chapter 3	Outbreak of War, 1939	44
Chapter 4	Learning to Fly, 1942	57
Chapter 5	Taking-off, 1943	73
Chapter 6	Prisoner of War, 1943	95
Chapter 7	Life in the Lager, 1943 – 1945	102
Epilogue	Life in Peacetime, 1945 – 2007	131
Picture credits		139

1

A KINGSBRIDGE CHILDHOOD
1920 – 1937

My father, Ernest Charles Warren, was born in Newton Abbot, Devon, where his father – my grandfather – was a master joiner and coffin maker. They lived at 72 Wolborough Street, and I remember the house had a massive garden at the back running up to a lane.

My father's mother had one leg amputated below the knee, after she got a splinter in her leg which became infected. She would get around the house by using a wheeled kitchen chair to support the stump as she whizzed about on the concrete floor. When she died Grandfather Warren, who had been ill for some time, married the young woman who had nursed him, much to the consternation of the family. She was rumoured to have been the widow of a sea captain, and she supposedly drank a bottle of gin a day. Eventually Grandfather Warren and his second wife sold the house in Wolborough Street and bought a bungalow at Kingsteignton; I remember spending a week with them when I was quite young.

My father had three brothers and a sister, although we didn't have much contact with them. Tom and Louis emigrated to Canada where Louis drifted from job to job, and Tom became an inspector on the Canadian Pacific Railways. Tom retired early and brought his wife Gertrude back to live in Newton Abbot where he took up a job as market manager for the town. Neither Tom or Louis had any children. The third brother, Arthur, was the rating officer for Newton Abbot, and he and his wife Winifred had three children

– my cousins Reg, Joan and Phyllis. When Winifred died Arthur married again and another cousin was born, David. Their sister Dolly had two sons, Brian who died from meningitis and Graham. Dolly took the surname Gerry but nobody knew anything about Mr Gerry.

My mother was called Florence Annie Whitting. She spent her whole life in Kingsbridge. Her father, my maternal grandfather, was William Whitting – always pronounced and spelt Whiting. Grampy, as we called him, owned Garden Mill Farm, Kingsbridge. Part of the farm was a swamp known as Whiting's Marsh, which is now the recreation ground. Grampy had a haulage business using horses and carts, traps and a huge eight-horse pantechnicon.

My father spent the greater part of the First World War in the Seaforth Highlanders, a Scottish regiment serving in India. I was born on 10 April, 1920, in a house on the quay at Kingsbridge, South Devon, and was later followed by my sister Una and brother Alan. In those days the quay area was very different, the estuary waters reaching the road at the bottom of the town. Wooden barges came right up to the rough ground where there was a public weighbridge, a big steel platform and a stone shed.

Once a year Roland & Anderton's Fair pitched on this area of gravel and ashes which was nearly opposite our house. During Fair Week, as I lay in bed I could hear the steam organ and see the lights from the Galloping Horses roundabout flashing around my bedroom.

Across the road from the house was a grand statue of Queen Victoria, above a water fountain which fed a double-sided water trough for horses, while on the south side was a smaller trough for dogs. I remember climbing up and sitting on the edge of the lower trough with my feet in the water on hot summer days. The Fountain was a striking and ornate edifice in sandstone topped with a large gas streetlamp. Sadly it was later removed to make way for new road junctions.

The top end of the quay area was fenced off from the road with granite posts and square iron bars between them. I once tried tightrope-walking on the bars but my feet slipped and my legs fell either side of the bar. I was carried back to my house writhing in pain – a shocking sensation I was to remember years later, when my parachute opened violently after an agonizing delay.

Grampy's farm

Looking at Kingsbridge quay and estuary today, filled with modern developments, it's difficult to picture the scene as it was in my childhood. On the west side of the estuary there was a narrow lane which was a short-cut to the market. Further down, where the car park is now, there was a timber yard and saw mill. Close by was our orchard, which Grampy rented from Colonel Ilbert of Bowringsleigh, and inside the gate was a large galvanised shed where we kept pigs, chickens and ducks. At the far end we had a vegetable garden and just outside was a massive pear tree about 30ft high which produced hundreds of sweet juicy pears.

The Colonel eventually wanted to sell the land for building development, and today it is the site of the old peoples' home. Grampy moved all the stock down to Tacket Wood which had a disused lime kiln in the bottom corner – this became our piggery. Part of the field was extremely steep, and on frosty moonlit evenings we would run down before tea and pour buckets of water from the cattle trough over the steepest slope. By the time we had finished our meal it would be frozen. We made all kinds of toboggans; one I used was an Coleman's mustard wall sign made of enamelled metal (and probably worth good money now), which was very fast but had a tendency to spin round and round.

I spent most of my early years with Grampy on the farm. When I got bigger and stronger I used to help castrate the pigs. I held them by the hind legs, head down, while Grampy castrated them. When he'd finished he used an old pudding basin full with brine to sterilise the wounds. When I let them go they would race across the field trying to get away from their own back ends.

The farmyard was in Union Road. There were stables with stalls for six horses, and a hayloft above with a chaff cutter. Next to the hayloft was a small room with a Petter engine, with a belt running up through a hole to the chaff cutter in the loft – Grampy had three badly-twisted fingers on his right hand as a result of an accident with the cutter. Next to the stables was a loose box, then a cart-and-trap shed with double doors. Further down the yard was a large barn which housed carts and wagons, the pantechnicon and a big pile of straw for bedding.

Along the bottom of the yard ran the cowsheds, where we housed our herd of Guernseys. When we were babies we were given milk from a newly-calved cow and kept to that same cow's milk in order not to upset our stomachs. Gran had a dairy in our house on the quay from where she sold milk, clotted cream, butter and hog's pudding.

In the yard was a handpump for water, piles of sand and the water sprinkler. This was a horse-drawn tank which held about 500 gallons with an 8ft-wide sprinkler at the back, operated by a lever. Grampy had the contract to water the Kingsbridge streets during the summer months, when one of his carters would drive around town, damping down the dust.

Union Road was very busy in the 1930s. On the corner, where it joined Mill Street, was a grain store. Further along was the Kingsbridge Brewery and the Gas Works where they made gas from coal. One of the by-products was tar, or 'poor man's black varnish' which we used to paint our galvanised iron roofs and sheds. About a quarter of a mile up the road was a huge building – the Workhouse. Children from the families in the Workhouse went to the local schools, led there and fetched every day by a rather simple inmate called Bert.

We had several more fields and a vegetable garden in a lane up past the Workhouse. I was up there on my pony one day, feeling hungry, so I tied the pony out in the lane and went over the hedge. I was feasting on peas, hidden down between the rows, when I heard Grampy's voice booming out: 'I know you're there, you little devil!' I guess the pony was a giveaway.

Market Day and Fair Day

Market Day in Kingsbridge meant herding cattle, sheep and horses from their farms, sometimes miles away, along the roads and tracks leading into town to be bought and sold. On occasions, when the tide was high, animals approaching along the banks of the estuary would wander deep into the water, and the drovers had to throw stones at them to make them swim towards the only slipway, near the public toilets.

Below the road, which is also a bridge, two tunnels about four feet high drained the brook that ran down beneath the town. One day, when the tide was out, two sheep on their way to market jumped off the wall and ran up one of the tunnels. One of the drovers went up after them but only succeeded in driving them even further up the tunnel. The tide came in and filled the tunnels. Days later two bloated corpses floated out.

Kingsbridge Fair Day was always on a Thursday in July. The night before, a garlanded glove was hung outside the Town Hall where it stayed for three days. As long as the glove and flowers were up, no-one could be summoned by the police for drunken behaviour or merrymaking – the tradition continues to this day.

On Fair Market Day farmers would set off in the early hours of the morning in order to get the best pens; the field just outside the market was covered in pens made of hurdles and nobody wanted to be last. We boys used to get out early and help to drive the sheep to earn some Fair money. There was chaos sometimes when two flocks met, with a lot of shouting, swearing and dogs barking.

On ordinary market days a lot of animals would be driven to the railway station to be loaded into box wagons or high-sided open-top wagons. Pigs of all sizes were driven, perhaps sixty or more, from the market to the station. The main pig drover was Tommy Luckes, and I remember one day as we were going up to the station yard, a big sow suddenly turned around and ran between Tommy's legs, lifted him off his feet and galloped back down the road with Tommy riding her facing backwards, shouting blue murder and waving his stick until he fell off. We laughed for weeks over that.

One day Grampy decided to take a sow to market in Newton Abbot as they fetched a better price there. In those days you transported pigs in an open cart with a net over the back. Between Totnes and Newton Abbot the road passes over the railway line, and just as Grampy got there a train came along. The horse had never seen a train before, let alone been surrounded with billowing steam and smoke, and it reared up, tipping the pig out of the cart, and then it bolted up the road. The terrified pig ran off in the opposite direction. It took quite a while for Grampy to reunite the pig – which luckily ran into a farm – with the horse and cart, by which time it was too late for the market, so he had to come home.

Horses and haulage

Grampy's haulage business was done by shire and Clydesdale cart horses. The pantechnicon, or furniture wagon, was drawn by six horses. I remember Grampy telling me about a load of furniture he had to deliver to Chagford. Coming out of Ashburton there's a steep hill called Halshanger Hill which leads up to Dartmoor. On reaching the top he stopped to ask a local chap directions to Chagford, but this led him miles out of the way. When he finally got there the horses were exhausted so Grampy stayed overnight at a coaching inn called the *Crown*.

Many years later, when I was living and teaching at Chagford, I met an old man in his 80s and he told me he used to live in Kingsbridge and his family moved up to Chagford when he was a youth. A man called Mr Whiting had brought their furniture in a horse-drawn huge pantechnicon.

Grampy had two-wheeled tipping carts which were used for unloading trains at the railway sidings, and barges and small tramp steamers at the quay. His men would deliver coal to coal yards, flour to bakers and cow-cake to agricultural merchants.

I was watching them down at the quay one day when the chief stevedore asked me if I had ever seen a cat play the bagpipes! When I laughed in disbelief he caught one of the ship's cats, held it head first, tight under his arm and bit its tail. The cat let out a yowl that sounded just like the bagpipes.

Grampy also dealt in horses and several people who knew him reckoned he was the only man they knew who could outdo a gypsy in a horse deal. He told me that if he was trying to sell a horse with 'broken wind' he would push lead balls into a block of lard and shove it down the horse's throat. This action disguised the condition for a few weeks! Grampy also took on difficult and rogue horses to re-train for other people. If he had a horse that kept rearing up for no reason he would carry a small thin glass bottle filled with warm water, and as soon as the horse reared up he smashed the bottle between its ears. The horse would think it had hit its head on a beam or tree branch and that the water was warm blood trickling down its face. After a few episodes it learned the lesson and would stop rearing.

One horse which was brought to Grampy had the habit of rearing up onto a wall with his forefeet and walking along sideways with his hind feet. He actually cured himself when he tried his wall-walking on a property with a 4ft wall surmounted by ornamental iron railings – he got stuck! Grampy had to jump off and run to the nearby *Ship and Plough* where unemployed men congregated in those days; it took four of them to lift the horse down.

In those days, when breaking in a horse they used to 'break his mouth' which meant putting on a tight belly-band to which was tied a rope on either side joined to a fierce bit in the mouth. The ropes were tightened so that the horse's head was pulled right in to his chest, and then he was left in a loose box all night. I had to let one out the next morning, and when I went in he was standing over a pile of foam, streaked with blood. As I led him out to have a drink from the water trough the belly-band got caught in the door catch, swinging the horse up against me and knocking the wind out of me. Poetic justice maybe.

Sometimes we had horses delivered by train. One evening four arrived, and Grampy and I went to the platformed siding to get them although it was getting dark. The porter, who was looking a bit anxious, said 'Go on boy, get in and get them out', but Grampy wouldn't hear of it. 'I'm not responsible for them until they are off the train' he said, 'they might trip or slip, anything could happen.' So the trembling porter had to get the horses out himself. We led

1. Bill's mother Florence ('Flo') and aunts Winifred ('Win') and Caroline ('Carrie'), with Grampy and Gran Whiting sitting.

2. Grampy Whiting

3. Grampy and Gran at the town house

4. Kingsbridge in the early 20th century, when schooners and paddle steamers carried goods and passengers to and from Plymouth. Grampy Whiting's land is on the left of the photograph.

Kingsbridge in the 1930s, when Bill Warren was a young boy.
5. (left) Fore Street.
6. (below) the quay.

7. Uncle Stan Perrott's store

8. Moysey's, owned by Bill's cousin's family

9. The annual steam fair on the quay, which young Bill could see from his bedroom window.

10. Kingsbridge market in 1930, held in the Ropewalk not far from Grampy's farmyard.

11. Bill with his father Ernest ('Ern')

12. Bill

13. Bill, four years old, with his sister Una, about six months

14. Kingsbridge carnival, mounted fancy dress parade; Bill as Pierrot on right.

15. Bill with cousin David Mosey, and Una on right

16. Ernie (left), Flo, Alan and Una (right), Bill sitting

17. Bill, aged about 10

18. Bill, grinning in the pale jacket, together with his parents, grandparents, uncles and aunts behind, sister Una on the left, and brother Alan and cousins in the foreground.

19. Bill at the beach with Una, right.

20. Kingsbridge Rugby XV, in 1914; Ernie Warren, Bill's father, in the front row, far right.

21. Kingsbridge Rugby XV, in the 1930s; Bill Warren in the second row, far right.

22. Camping with Bob Kerswill (left) at Bearscombe

BOXING

Promotion by Kingsbridge Rugby Football Club under
Licence from B.B.B. of C.)

TOWN HALL, KINGSBRIDGE
SATURDAY, MARCH 13th

Great Ten-Rounds Middle-Weight Contest
BILL HOOD v ALF UNDERWOOD
Cosmo Club   Plymouth

Great Eight-Rounds Fly-Weight Bout
TED SKINNER v. TICH HAMBLY
Cosmo Club   City Athletic Club

Four-Rounds Welter Contest
HARRY TRANT v. ERN HOLMAN
Kingsbridge   Cosmo Club

Four-Rounds Welter Bout
JOHN TRANT v. PHIL JUDE
Kingsbridge   Plymouth

Local Fights
Charlie Lockhart v. Bill Warren
Arthur Burgoyne v. Young Bourne, Modbury
Bill Burgoyne v. Fearnley Wotton (Salcombe)

Doors open 6.45 p.m.   Commence 8 p.m.
3,6   2/4   1/3 (including tax)
Get your Tickets at once from any member of the
R.F.C. Committee and avoid disappointment. Any
seat can be reserved. Phone 270.   5979

incident appeared wholly accidental, as both
boxers showed when Trant went across to
Jude to apologise.
    A return match between Charlie Lockhart
and Bill Warren resulted in the former re-
peating his victory of last month. In the
first two rounds the fight was even, and
neither could claim marked advantage, but
in the succeeding rounds Lockhart began to
use his left and right with effect, while
Warren could only use his left.
    The last two fights featured clashes
between Kingsbridge and Modbury, and
Kingsbridge and Salcombe, Kingsbridge
being represented by the Burgoyne brothers.

*Bill's return fight with Charlie Lockhart, as covered by the **Kingsbridge Gazette**, in March 1937.*

23. Charlie Lockhart (left) and Bill

24. Bill posing in the backyard, aged 16

them back to our stables overnight as two were for someone out Sherford way. We often did this, the farmer gave me a pony for my reward later on.

I often had to drive a horse and cart out to the beach at Thurlestone, a distance of about four miles. Grampy paid a man who lived near the beach to load the cart with sand for me. Coming back was alright until we got to the top of West Alvington Hill which was steep and even worse as we got near the station. At the top of the hill I would stop and apply a drogue to one wheel which acted as a brake. The drogue was a small steel sledge, the width of the cart wheel rim, and I had to place it in front of the wheel, then move the horse on a bit to get the wheel on top of the drogue, and keep the horse still while I chained it in place. This had the effect of stopping one wheel turning which slowed the cart down. The result was a burn mark on the road as friction caused the drogue to get red hot. Even so, where the road was really steep the horse would slip and slide down the hill.

A horse would collapse if the weight was too great, then it would have to be cut out of its harness. This never happened to any of our horses because Grampy always said 'Load light and come again!' Tarred roads were a great hazard for iron-shod horses, especially when the shoes were worn a bit; before I took a horse out to Thurlestone I'd go up to Harry Boundy the blacksmith and he'd put in a rough nail on both hind shoes - a nail with its head sticking out. If we did a lot of roadwork we'd get him to put in Mortegg studs which had very hard heads.

One day I was walking up Fore Street when a gypsy came down with a small pony pulling an overloaded trap. The chap was pushing back on the shaft trying to stop the pony and trap sliding on down the hill, when suddenly the doctor's wife rushed at him, hitting him across the head with her handbag! 'You cruel man!

This poor pony is overloaded!' she shouted, while the poor chap tried to hold back the trap and protect his head at the same time.

Bearscombe Farm

I used to spend a lot of time at Bearscombe Farm with my friend Bob Kerswell. I often rode my pony out there after school on a Friday and stayed until Sunday afternoon. When we were younger we used to keep newts, and made little carts from matchboxes, tying a couple of newts on the front with cotton harnesses. One of the newts died, so we decided to give it a proper burial. We placed it carefully in the matchbox cart and, deciding it was a three-newt load, we harnessed up three newts to the hearse. The solemn procession to the grave failed miserably when the three pulling the hearse shot off in different directions tipping over the cart.

When it was wet we moved into an old chicken shed with a magic lantern. We hung an old sheet on the wall as the screen, the lantern was a box with a lens set in one side and a slot to insert glass slides all illuminated by a candle at the back. We were mesmerised by such amazing things as volcanoes, mountains and icebergs.

In the winter the cart horses, especially the shires with their heavy feathering, would develop 'sweet itch' and 'greasy heel' so every Sunday morning Bob and I would ride them down to the meadow and take them up through the stream at the bottom. I was riding an old mare called Diamond one Sunday, and I didn't think she was moving fast enough over the stony bottom of the stream so I picked a stick and gave her a tickle. She shot forward suddenly and went down in the stream throwing me up onto her head with my left leg stuck under her shoulder. The stream was running pretty high and although I could get my head above water, Diamond couldn't! Luckily, this all happened where the bank widened slightly, giving me the chance to throw myself into the riverside bushes and allowing Diamond to lift her head out of the water and get up. She galloped all the way back to the farm and straight into her stall in the stables. I doubled-up and rode back to the farm with Bob to find that Mrs Kerswell had run a hot bath for me, it was such a freezing cold morning.

During one summer Bob and I spent most nights sleeping in our camp down in the meadow – a shack made from rustic poles covered with tarpaulins. The Haddys, on the next farm, had a very bad-tempered bull which had smashed through several gates and got loose a few times. There was only an old barbed wire fence on their side of our camp and the stream on our side. One night we were woken by a noise outside; I looked out and said to Bob 'I thought there were three cows and a horse out there, now there are five shapes in the field'. 'That's Haddy's bull got across! Keep quiet or he'll knock this place to smithereens and us with it!' All night one of us would whisper 'You awake?' and the other would reply 'Yes, shhhh!' Next morning we found Mr Kerswell had put another cow in the field after we had gone to sleep!

Bob had a nanny goat which was a bit wild. She had twin kids and when they grew a bit they escaped and became feral, often to be seen roaming over all the farms in the district. One day when I arrived Bob said 'Come on, those damn goats are up in Higher Barrs!' We got the sheepdog, thinking we could get them cornered. What a hope! They went down across Barrs and over the hedge with a big drop down to the road below. We ran down thinking there would be injured goats in the road, but there was nothing! Later we saw them going up across Ranscombe's fields.

We had some sheep penned in the lane outside the house. I held each one and Bob shot tablets down their throats. One was particularly lively and I laughed when Bob said 'Hold onto him 'til he uses his yucker!'

One day Bob's father was going up to feed the sheep with a bag of flaked maize. He was going to ride on the old pony they got from 'Pig Killer' Stone. He put the bag on the pony and got on it himself. Bob gave the pony a whack and shouted 'Get on!' The pony ran forward, tripped over Scot, the old blind sheepdog, and went down on his knees. The dog set up a terrible howling and Mr Kerswell came half off the pony. He had one foot hopping around on the ground and the other caught up on the pony's withers and he was shouting 'Whoa, whoa!' Bill Payne, who was with us, thought the dog was after him so he ran into the barn and shut the door. Meanwhile Bob and I were helpless with laughter, and for a long time afterwards we'd crack up again whenever someone shouted 'Whoa, whoa!'

They also had a donkey at Bearscombe; it went out with the cows, and was supposed to stop them 'slipping' a calf. We used to get on the donkey in turn while the other one shoved a bit of holly branch between his hind legs to make him buck. The one who stayed on longest was the winner. The donkey seemed to join in the fun. Another time we found an old piece of inner tube and decided to go rabbiting. Bob set fire to the tube in the rabbit hole on one side of the hedge and I was out the other side with a stick waiting for the rabbits to bolt. Nothing! After several more attempts we gave up. When we got back Bob's father said 'No wonder they didn't bolt, the rabbits were all sitting there enjoying the warmth from the burning rubber'.

Bob used to set mole traps, he'd skin them and sell the pelts for fourpence each – a third of the price of 20 Players cigarettes in those days. Johnnie Damerall, who lived at Bowcombe, also set traps and Bob would often discover his traps empty and little signs that they had been emptied and re-set. I used to tease him that

Johnnie was a better mole-catcher than he was because he caught his own and Bob's too!

Those were the days when old Mrs Rutt used to come round with a pony and open cart, loaded with crabs and strings of a dozen sandeels. The crabs were fourpence each (a farm labourer's weekly wage was 32 shillings at that time). The sandeels were soused in vinegar or fried a golden-brown.

As boys we used to fish for smelts over the bridge at Bowcombe about a mile out of town. These were eight or nine inches long and delicious when fried. We also gathered cockles and winkles from the estuary.

School days

When we were young we never stayed home. When the weather was good we'd be out in the fields miles away. Farmers used to fold the sheep on to turnips (swedes) so if we got hungry we'd take a swede, knock the skin off on a gatepost and have a snack. Farmers didn't mind if you took a couple of swedes home for dinner. We especially liked swede tops, after a frost, when they tasted like kale.

I used to hate school, I often got the cane which was usually given by the headmaster. You had to bend over with your fingers touching your toe-caps – if not you got one across the back of your hands, followed by three or six across the backside, each one leaving a mark.

We used to have gangs, and one night after school our gang got into a fight with another from 'Shanghai' – the nickname for the council housing estate. We were enjoying a good punch-up when a voice cried 'Stop this at once! I know you, Billy Warren!' It was the headmaster's wife, walking up with her shopping basket. She knew me, and only me, because we were both in the church choir. I knew I'd get it the next day at school so I stuck a piece of cardboard down the back of my trousers.

Sure enough, at assembly the headmaster called me up on the stage, gave a lecture about letting the school down and told me to bend over. When the first stroke descended there was an almighty whack, which sent my mates into fits of giggles as they knew what I had done. The headmaster wasn't too pleased, though. 'What have you got inside your trousers, boy?' I replied, 'A piece of cardboard, sir'. 'Take it out and we will start again'. I was the hero of the school that day, and my mates reckoned that the teachers on the stage had a job to keep from laughing. It didn't do me any good though, I got six of the best with increased acceleration!

Sometimes at the end of a lesson we were questioned on the facts we had learned, and a failure to answer resulted in three of the best. I had my fair share of these because I daydreamed whilst watching flies climbing up the windows and thinking about other things. However, it certainly made you learn and remember facts.

School discipline was very strict; before the morning and afternoon sessions when the bell went, we had to line up in military fashion, two deep. We responded to commands to form fours, form two deep, right or left dress, right turn, left turn etc. On the command 'Quick march' we marched across the yard and up the steps, where the headmaster would be standing, and gave him the 'eyes left' as we passed him, then marched on down more steps to the school – all the time keeping in step.

There were no school buses or dinners in those days, and children from far-off villages would walk to school in all weathers. At midday the teachers went home and locked the school, so the country kids had to eat their packed lunch – if they had one – sitting on a bench along the wall of a lean-to shed in the lower playground. During the dinner break the kids ran around playing all kinds of chasing games, which often resulted in fights, but it all helped to keep us warm in the winter months.

Riding adventures

I had a pony which was a cross between a New Forest and a thoroughbred, I used to ride it and lead two cart horses out to the fields at the end of the day. I remember how hard it was to open the gate and ride through still holding on to the carthorses, close the gate and tie my pony to it, holding on to the horses before releasing them one at a time, watching out for a kick back as they galloped away, glad to be free. Then I had to ride back to the stables for two more. Once I didn't tie the pony to the gate properly and it galloped all the way back to the stables with reins and stirrups flapping. I had to run the half-mile back to catch up with him.

I often took a carthorse up to be shod at the blacksmiths at the top of Fore Street. The smithy and riding stables were owned by George Kennard, whose son Les was a friend of mine. Les later became a well-known trainer of steeplechase horses.

One Sunday morning Les Kennard and I were down at the stables, where I was mucking out my pony which was tied outside. Les said he would go for a ride on her, but I warned him that she was a handful and not like a riding stables horse. However he put on the bridle and set off up the road riding bareback. After a short while I heard them coming at a full gallop, I rushed out with a dung fork in my hand to try and stop her but she started to slide and I had to jump out of the way or be knocked flying. She picked up her feet and galloped on, heading for the field to join the carthorses. As she got in to the town she had to negotiate a sharp left corner but she slipped up on her side. Les of course came off in a heap and suffered a badly-bruised and grazed arm and leg.

I managed to catch the pony and got her back in the stable, then took Les home. His father was furious: 'Don't you ever ride that pony again. It's not an ordinary pony – it's a pony and a half!'

She ran away with me several times, usually when there were horses behind. Once I was out hunting when she took off at a gallop, passed the huntsman and was up amongst the hounds before I could stop her. We tried everything to get her under control, including a fixed martingale, a curb chain and severe bits, added to my sawing at her mouth, but nothing worked. I just learned to hang on until she gave up.

An amusing thing happened when Les and I were hunting out near Frogmore. I was very keen on a girl called Grace Seymour who was a very good horsewoman. I was dying for a pee so I told Les to stand guard. We waited for all the hunt-followers to come through the field gate and then I turned my pony back through the gate. I was enjoying the relief of a pee when Grace came galloping back to see where I was! We were both very, very embarrassed, especially Grace who blushed very easily.

George Kennard, Les's father, used to keep horses in stables at Thurlestone during the summer months for visitors at the hotel to ride. The stables were owned by the Grose family who also owned the hotel. Les and I would often take fresh horses out and bring back the tired ones. We could ride one and lead two each, a thing you couldn't do these days down narrow country lanes. At that time there were very few vehicles on the roads and the sound of an engine up in the sky brought everyone out of their houses to see an aeroplane!

On Sunday mornings we used to go riding with my uncle Bill Elliot, Ralph Steer the baker, and a pig-headed bank clerk called Jobson. My uncle and I had our own horses and the others rented theirs from Kennard's riding school. There was a day when we were riding along the top of the beach at Thurlestone where the grass was full of rabbit holes. Jobson took off at a gallop and of course the other horses followed. We were going hell-for-leather when my uncle's horse put his foot in a hole and somersaulted, throwing him off. I was right behind and to avoid the fallen horse I had to jump an iron fence into a field. It took me ages to find a gate and join the rest, all of whom were fortunately unhurt. After a few choice words with Jobson we sorted ourselves out and went up a lane beside the Rock House Hotel, to go across fields back to South Milton. On the way up the lane Jobson's horse, which was known to be a head-shaker, brought her head up suddenly and smacked him hard in the teeth and nose, which then bled profusely, giving me a lot of satisfaction.

The eventful ride continued in the same vein. Going through a gate at the top of the lane Bill Elliot banged his knee painfully on the gatepost (afterwards he was unable to work for nearly a month with fluid on the knee). But that was not the end of our troubles, as we moved on across the fields we were attacked by six carthorses and we had to lash out at them to stop them biting and kicking our smaller steeds. We were all glad to finally get home that day.

The Croft Farm murders

When I was 16, in the summer of 1936, I often used to stay out at Bearscombe, and a gang of us would regularly cycle off to the local dance venue at Stokenham village, about six miles from Kingsbridge; if you wanted to meet with the best girls you had to be a good dancer in those days.

One night in June, I dallied a while after the dance, kissing a girlfriend, then got on my bike and set off towards Kingsbridge. As I came through Chillington, a chap I knew called Charlie Lockhart

– who had also been saying goodnight to another girl – shouted at me to hang on and wait for him. We cycled along together talking and in no hurry, as it was a really warm night even though it was after 2am. Charlie was older than me, and worked for the Maye family at Croft Farm, West Charleton, where he also lived. We parted at the end of his lane and I cycled on to Bearscombe where I happened to look at the clock – it was 2.40am.

The next morning I was in Fore Street, Kingsbridge, when I saw two smartly-dressed men talking to some local people who were pointing at me. The strangers came over and asked my name and introduced themselves as a detective inspector and a sergeant. It transpired that on leaving me the previous night, Charlie had reached the farmhouse and on going upstairs he found one of the daughters on the first landing covered in blood and groaning. He rushed up to the next landing were he found the farmer's wife and the second daughter both dead with their heads savagely beaten in. The smell of smoke drew him to a bedroom where the farmer was lying on the bed drenched in paraffin, and alight, with the dog beside him. Charlie rushed down to the kitchen to get a fire extinguisher and managed to put the flames out. He then ran to the post office, opposite the end of the farm lane, banged on the door and woke the postmaster, who then rang the police.

The two policemen took me and my bike in a van back to the end of the lane leading to the farm which was the scene of the tragedy. I had to ride from there to Bearscombe at the same speed as I'd ridden it the night before while they checked the time.

Months later, when the trial came to court, I was called to attend. I remember sitting in an office under the Town Hall, and the farmer was sitting at a table eating roast lamb and mint sauce, unaware of my presence. His name was Thomas Maye and he was a very religious and respected member of the community. I wasn't required to give evidence in the end, and Maye was charged with murder; it was thought he suffered some kind of 'brainstorm' [Maye was acquitted at the judge's direction after a doctor maintained that the farmer's injuries could not have been self-inflicted]. Rumour had it that, some months before all this, a film unit had been working out at Torcross and Beesands and one of his daughters had an affair with a member of the film crew and became pregnant. Anyway, it seems that my evidence put Charlie in the clear.

It was some time before I encountered Charlie again, and this time we weren't dancing with girls but instead dancing around a boxing ring. A few of us had set up a boxing club at Bearscombe, rigging up a rope ring in a disused granary with a hurricane lamp at each corner for illumination. The trouble was there were so many shadows you didn't know which was a punch and which was a shadow. In February 1937, when I was still a couple of months away from my 17th birthday, a fight was arranged for me at the Town Hall. My opponent was Charlie, who was now a man of 26. By the last round I was well ahead on points; we were both covered in blood, mostly his. He caught me with a haymaker and I went down for a count of eight and finished the round on my feet but the referee gave the decision to him. My second was a professional boxer from Plymouth, and he wasn't too happy with the amateur ref's decision – he was sure I had won on points.

A return fight was arranged a month later, on 13 March 1937, billed with the title 'Remember their last fight?' This time, in the second round, I dislocated my righthand thumb, and it was so painful I could only deliberately miss, or pull, my righthand punches. After the fight – which of course I lost – the First Aid chaps sent me across to the doctor who should have been at the ringside. I had to wait in the lounge with a box of chocolates while he finished his dinner before he relocated and strapped my thumb.

Work as a Post Office engineer

I finally escaped from school and was pushed into a job with the Post Office – I say 'pushed' because the creepy old boy who did Grampy's accounts was the employment officer and between them they decided it was a marvellous opportunity. I was accepted and sat an exam, scoring high enough marks to enter the engineering department. I didn't like it much; learning about ohms and amps didn't seem to bring forth a spark of interest in me! At this time I also realised I had wasted a lot of time at school so I did a correspondence course from one of the universities. However, I did enjoy working with the telephone engineers as all the work was out in the countryside.

I started off working with an old jointer called Jim Hannaford, a friend of our family. Our job was to find faults in the overhead lead cables, using a machine they called a 'megger' – a nickname for megohmeter. You turned the handle, gradually building up speed, to produce an electric current; you could then read off on the dial approximately how far away the fault was in yards. My paces were exactly one yard and sometimes we found the fault very quickly, but at other times it took all day because the fault might be a mere crack in the lead sleeve letting in water, or even just damp air. If we discovered the fault in the morning, Jim would say 'Right, boy, drive into that field' and we'd spend most of the day sunbathing and making tea or warming our pasties in a little stove he'd made, heated by our blow lamp. Eventually, in the afternoon, he'd say 'Well, I suppose we'd better repair that fault now.'

Quite often we went to an old listening site vacated by the RAF at East Prawle. It was locked and fenced but we had the key as a lot of our cables went through there. If the inspector came up from Plymouth to check us he had to blow his horn to be let in, so of course by then we'd be working hard.

During this time I made a friend of Tom Jackson who came to work at the Kingsbridge telephone exchange as a linesman. Tom had been brought up in the West Indies where his father was an agricultural advisor, and first came to England when he was 19. Tom had heard stories about dangerous encounters with bulls, and one day we were out shooting in Bearscombe Wood, when we came to a three-cornered field. Tom crept up a narrow path on one side, between a thicket of brambles and the boundary hedge, whilst I climbed the steep field to meet him at the top corner. As luck would have it there was a steer feeding in the top path; it must have been half-asleep as I crept up behind it and gave a yell, booting it up the backside at the same time. Tom was coming up the narrow path and suddenly saw the steer running downhill, thought it was a bull and turned tail as fast as he could run. I ran back out into the field in time to see Tom breaking all speed records with both hands on his pockets to stop the cartridges from flapping. When I finally caught up with him I couldn't speak for laughing!

Tom got his own back when we were out shooting again at a later date. Bob's father had asked me to feed his steers in the field we were crossing; the fattening cake was stored in a metal bin against the hedge and they fed from metal troughs. The steers all crowded around us and I said 'Which one do you want me to ride?' He replied 'The biggest one of course!" I squeezed between them and as I jumped on the largest of the South Devons it jumped over the trough and I went across the field with my right knee over its back and my left leg trailing. Soon I felt a bang on my knee which knocked me off. The knee started to swell badly and took a couple of weeks to heal before I could return to work.

2

AIRMAN, SECOND CLASS
1938

Leading up to 1938 the situation in Germany had been getting steadily worse, and of great concern to Europe and Britain in particular. War seemed to be imminent, and my father and uncles thought that I should join up before it became compulsory, giving me time to get trained for conflict. I decided to join the RAF, and I applied at the recruiting office in Plymouth, where I took a written examination and a mathematics paper, both of which were quite easy. There were five other blokes there and we were given the papers and left alone in a room to answer the questions. The others were able to ask for my help with spellings and maths, so we all passed.

Some weeks later, in October 1938, I received a rail warrant for travel to RAF West Drayton, quite close to where Heathrow airport is now. I remember it being a dark, small dump of a place. After a day or two getting fitted out with uniforms and other formalities, I became an airman, 2nd class. About twenty of us were posted to the big initial training centre at Cardington, just outside Bedford. The days here were spent in drilling, PE and various lectures. We weren't allowed out of camp during the week but given passes on Saturdays and Sundays from 12 noon until 9.30pm.

When the wind was in the right direction the smell of farmyard manure wafted across the parade ground from a nearby farm, which made me feel quite homesick. I also found the 'bull' in this camp hard to handle. I'm surprised the NCOs didn't sprout horns! On Friday nights we had to scrub the wooden floor of our barrack room with soap and water. Later they moved us out and laid linoleum, dark brown, but that had to be scrubbed with paraffin to remove the black marks left by rubber gym shoes. Each hut had a 'Tortoise' stove which needed to be black-lead polished – including the chimney. The brass window catches and coal scuttle also had to be polished. When all the room chores were finished we had to start on our kit. Belts, straps, backpack and pouches all had to be 'Blanco'd' with a white paste out of a large tin. Next, all the brass buttons and buckles were cleaned and polished until they sparkled. The Saturday morning parade was in full uniform with all equipment for careful inspection; the slightest hint of Blanco on the brass, or Brasso on the straps, and you had to take it all off and a sergeant would stamp all over it to make sure you spent Saturday afternoon re-cleaning the lot while the rest of the chaps went out.

One Friday night a chap in our hut called Smith – a scruffy lazy so-and-so – instead of doing his share of the cleaning, said he had to make a phone call and he didn't come back for an hour or more. We found out later he was in the NAAFI all the time. The following Friday he slipped off and again didn't come back until the work was done.

'Hello Smithy, your glasses are a bit bent', I said. He took them off and immediately all 20 of us piled in, stripped him naked and covered him with stove black from head to foot. The latrines were outside and were quite primitive with concrete floors and a wall tap for filling buckets. Smithy was carried out, protesting loudly, and held under the tap and scrubbed almost clean. The experience was enough to ensure that he did his share of the Friday night cleaning thereafter.

Cardington had been the base for airships, the R100 and R101, in the 1930s. The towers to which they had been anchored were still there, as were the two massive hangars where they had been garaged. We played rugby on the airfield but when it was too wet we had an indoor pitch marked out in the hangars where we played 'touch rugby' because the ground was concrete. Sometimes when we were playing outside the hangars a klaxon would warn us of an incoming aircraft, usually an old Vickers Vimy bi-plane bomber, but these were so heavy and slow we had up to ten minutes before it landed. We would pull up the goalposts, wait until it touched down and then put the posts back again and carry on with the game.

Chaps from the westcountry seemed to stick together, and one of my main mates was from Honicknowle, Plymouth. Len Huck and I got posted together several times. He was a keen cross-country runner and every evening he'd run around the whole airfield. He kept on about the number of rabbits there were at the extreme perimeter where nobody went. I got hold of some wire and made a few snares and instructed him exactly how to set them.

After two or three days he came back in the evening and told me there was a dead rabbit in one of the snares. I told him to fetch it but he was worried about how he could conceal it when he was only wearing PE kit. 'Put on a jacket and if anyone stops you, say you have a cold,' I suggested. 'Tie the rabbit's back legs with string and hang it round your neck so it's inside your tunic out of sight.'

Later he returned with the rabbit after encountering an officer on his way through the camp. As he lifted his arm to salute, the tunic rose and exposed the rabbit's head! Len held his breath in panic but the flight lieutenant laughed and walked on chuckling. We took the rabbit to the next hut where the cooks and butchers were billeted; as we moved along the line to collect our brown stew at supper they reached under the counter and we both had a piece of rabbit.

There was generally friendly rivalry between huts although that didn't rule out practical jokes. At the back of each hut was a porch, with the mains switch for all the lights. Creeping up in the dark, switching off the lights then making a run for it was a bit obvious. Our hut went one better. I was lifted up onto the flat roof of the next hut where I could lie and reach out to pull the lever of the fuse box. The first time I did it I could hear a lot of swearing as they fumbled their way out in the dark, but of course they saw no one there, so they switched on the lights and went back inside. I waited until they were settled down and then switched off again. I heard them discussing the next move, 'We'll stay just inside the door and rush out before they can run away!' I waited a long time but of course they still found nobody in sight. I listened to their discussions below me, until eventually they realised that I must be on the roof. My mates leapt out of hiding and got me down just in time, otherwise my punishment would probably have been 'blacking out' with stove black.

On Sunday mornings we had to go on Church Parade, marching up to the big hut which served as a church for Sunday service. If you said you were an atheist, or followed some other religion, you stood outside in lines at attention throughout the service, no matter what the weather. We all went inside as it was warmer!

When we finished our initial training we had to choose the trade we were to follow. As I had been a Post Office engineer I was pushed into training as a wireless operator and I was posted to Yatesbury on the Wiltshire Downs.

RAF Yatesbury

We travelled from Bedford to Calne by train, and were met at the station by RAF lorries. When we arrived at Yatesbury we jumped down from the back of the lorry into a sea of mud. The camp was only half built! It was a dreadful place, miles from anywhere, with nothing to do out of training time.

At weekends about 30 of us would walk up onto the Downs, find a wide open area, and creep around spread out in a circle. At a given signal we quietly and slowly closed the circle to trap some of the scores of hares that inhabited the Downs. Then the fun began as we tried to catch them. We never succeeded but it gave us plenty of exercise and a great deal of amusement.

My best mate at Yatesbury was a chap called Jack Hooker. We both played for the station 1st Rugby 15. He and I would go out over the Downs on Sunday afternoons if there was nothing else to do; even in deep snow, it was good to get out of the camp sometimes. When we could afford it we walked about two miles down the road to Beckhampton to a pub called the *Wagon and Horses*. The famous Fred Darling racing stables were in Beckhampton and we got friendly with some of the stable lads who drank at the pub, and who sometimes gave us a good tip! I was going on leave once and one of the lads gave me a couple of good horses to back. When I got back to Kingsbridge I put a ten-shilling double on them both and then forgot all about it. Several days later I remembered and checked up to find they had both won and I collected £20 in winnings!

After several weeks on the Wireless Ops Course most of us hated it. Every day we had to learn and practise the Morse Code which was boring in the extreme. We also had to learn all the technical side of radio receiving. At the end of the course we had to be able to send and receive messages at over 20 words a minute. Six or eight of us decided we would deliberately fail the final exams. I thought there might be trouble over this, so I pretended I couldn't get more than 12 words a minute although in reality I could do more than 20. A few of the chaps gave silly answers to some of the technical questions: 'What precautions would you take when changing an accumulator?' Answer: 'On no account let the moon shine on it'. The CO was not pleased. I did well on the technical paper but to my dismay he gave me another month to try and get my Morse up to speed. At the end of the month I was no better so I was failed. There were several of us failures waiting to be posted elsewhere. I opted for general duties but we seemed like the lost tribe, no training, no daily parade, nothing we had to do so we got a bit slack.

This came to a head when the station warrant officer suddenly called us outside to line up for a kit inspection. I heard him ask several of the men when they had cleaned their buttons last, and they all replied, 'Yesterday, sir', whereupon he became apoplectic. I decided it was no good lying so I replied 'Last week, sir' and that was the last straw. He reckoned I was insubordinate and put me on a charge. I was confined to camp for a week and each evening I had to report in full kit and double around the square with a PE corporal shouting at me to keep going.

Sometime before all this Jack Hooker and I had discussed deserting – making our way to Bristol and working our way to South America. Luckily our plans came to nothing, and I got posted to the newly-opened technical training station at RAF Locking, in Weston-super-Mare.

3

OUTBREAK OF WAR
1939

My first duties at Locking were in the camp office, and I met up with Len Huck again; we had both been promoted to corporal at the same time. Off-duty we went into Weston to the pubs where the locals usually ignored us. But on the night that we heard the announcement of Britain's entry into the war on the hut radio, our reception at the pub was very different. The locals were all over us trying to buy us drinks. I was 19 years old and had no idea what the final outcome of that night might be.

Our station CO was a squadron leader [Group Captain James McCrae] and a really decent chap. He told me that he had been in the Egyptian Police before the war. At Christmas that year the CO said 'Come on, let's go out and get Xmas trees. We need three, one each for the men's, the sergeants' and the officers' mess.' Off we went in a truck down the country lanes to a plantation he knew about. When I asked if he had permission, he said 'No, keep quiet and be ready to run.' We had cut three nice trees and thrown them over the fence when we heard a noise, so we got out quickly, loaded the trees, and the CO drove off like a scalded cat. We were driving up a lane just wide enough for the truck when round a corner we were confronted by a column of marching soldiers. I have never seen men jump so quickly; in unison, they all jumped up in the hedges and hung on for dear life. The CO exclaimed 'Christ, that was a near one – but then they were only soldiers!'

Just before Christmas (1939) I was called on again by the CO, this time to take a lorry and driver to the brewery at Weston and collect some booze for the festive period. The manager told one of his men to look after the driver while he showed me around the brewery. I remember sampling drinks taken from the biggest sherry barrel I had ever seen. When the lorry was loaded we drove back to camp and delivered the booze to each mess; there were crates and crates of bottles and barrels of beer. After checking the lists for each mess, I discovered there was a bottle of gin going spare. I called the senior NCOs together and we sat on my bunk and finished the bottle off.

By now Len and I were sergeants, each in charge of a 'wing'. Every morning the troops paraded on the square for the Raising of the Flag ceremony. We then marched them back to the huts for inspection; the huts had to be clean, tidy and equipment laid out correctly and in perfect condition. A corporal stood beside me with a notebook, recording any faults, and offenders were brought to me after inspection for a tongue-lashing.

One morning there was a senior NCOs' meeting. The sergeants had to draw lots to decide who would muster the troops for morning parade. Len and I drew the lowest numbers and so lost. There we were, he with 600 troops on one side of the huge parade ground and me with the same number on the other side. Len and I stood back-to-back in the middle of the square giving them the usual 'Quick march, left turn, right turn, form fours' etc. As time went on we chatted a bit in between orders, until Len suddenly screamed 'Look at your troops!' I had failed to 'about turn' them and the first ranks were marching across the perimeter road and over the garden in front of the CO's office. I hurriedly yelled 'About turn! Halt!' I then got the eight men nearest the garden to repair the damage. Fortunately the CO was away for a few days so everything was OK.

Len became the proud owner of a motorbike which was good news for the three of us who hung about together in our spare time. If we went to Weston, Len drove the bike and the other two took turns on the pillion or the handlebars. The road into Weston from the camp crossed a humped-back bridge over the railway line, and the thrill was to try and become airborne which occasionally we did! Sometimes poor old Len rode the bike home with Frank on the handlebars and me on the pillion, both of us eating fish and chips and feeding Len as we went.

I got a bit suspicious of a certain bugler who was supposed to blow Reveille at two points on the campsite where the roads crossed. One morning I got up early and dressed, because I thought the sound of his bugle wasn't coming from either of the crossroads. I found him still in his pyjamas leaning out of the hut window – another candidate for a good tongue-lashing.

As a sergeant I was often sent out on various missions, such as escorting 60 airmen from Locking to Skegness where they would start their next training course. I handed them over and as I had a long wait for a train back to Weston I wandered out to the sea-front. At intervals along the beach were soldiers stationed with machine guns pointing out to sea in case there were low-level attacks by German bombers. I got talking to one of the squaddies about his machine gun, as I hadn't come across that model before. He was keen to show me exactly how it worked, but as he released the safety catch the thought went through my head 'if he touches the trigger now…boom!' And he did! He jumped backwards, scared white, whilst I made myself scarce, looking back to see sergeants and officers running to try and see the approaching aircraft.

On another occasion I had to select two airmen as escorts to take a prisoner to the 'glasshouse' at Shepton Mallet. He was a Maltese airman, crazy as a loon. I didn't handcuff him because

I had a Smith & Wesson 44 and a rifle, and I told him I would shoot him if there was any nonsense. On the train journey the two escorts were telling him that the glasshouse supplied girls and he would be let out once a week to go to the pictures. When we got off the train there was a fair distance to walk through the streets and he was shouting at women all the way. Apparently the night before we picked him up, he was locked in the armoury which had a very solid door and he had nearly smashed through it with his head! When we arrived at the glasshouse everything was done at the double, so we had to double around with him until I handed him over.

Another horrible trip was the time I took two airmen up to Winson Green Prison, in the centre of Birmingham, to bring back a persistent deserter called Eagles; the CO told me he didn't trust the service police and that he would rather I did it. In front of us in the queue at the check-out desk was an older army sergeant and four escorts, signing out two deserters. I had to laugh when he slammed the bolt of his rifle shut with a bullet up the breach and turned to his prisoners and said 'Did you see that? I signed for two bodies which I'm taking back to camp. It's up to you whether your souls go back with them.'

My prisoner was a slimy customer with the gift of the gab, so I handcuffed him to one of my escorts. We had to cross London by taxi, and when we got to Paddington station it was late evening and he kept on saying 'Come on, sarge, my sister lives in the East End, we could stay the night there and you could sleep with her'. I told the escort attached to him 'every time he talks nonsense like that yank the handcuff on his wrist hard'. We finally got on the train and left London but when we reached the outskirts of Bristol the train stopped at an outlying station – there was an air raid in progress. We disembarked and a coach took us right around Bristol to board another train on the other side of the city. This was all I needed! I put another handcuff on the prisoner and attached him to my left wrist, leaving my right wrist free to hold my Smith & Wesson, and when he started to fight back I got the other escort to sit on him! When we eventually arrived back at Weston there was a lorry waiting to take us back to camp. I was glad to hand him over to the CO!

The evacuation of troops from Dunkirk in June 1940 saw a huge influx of soldiers needing temporary accommodation at RAF Locking. Some were in a terrible way; they hadn't had their boots off for over a month, and when their footwear was cut off their feet were in a pretty bad state.

One night I was sitting outside the offices in a deckchair with the station CO when suddenly we heard and then caught sight of the first German bombers, on their way to bomb Bristol [throughout the summer and autumn of 1940 there were sporadic enemy attacks on Bristol, Avonmouth and the surrounding area, including Weston, and Bristol's first Blitz took place on 24 November]. On some nights each sergeant had to take ten men and we would be dropped off in the city during, or right after, an air raid. We saw horrendous sights as we helped clear buildings of concrete, bricks and timber to reach the people trapped beneath; some were dead, others severely injured or close to death.

Some of us senior NCOs were billeted out in Weston, partly to give the locals a bit of reassurance and partly because the camp was getting very crowded; I was billeted with a lay preacher, his wife and son. I remember one night I was walking home from the pub when I heard the engines of enemy aircraft, then the sound of bombs dropping nearby. Just as I opened the front door a bomb exploded very close, and the preacher came flying down the stairs, slipped up sideways on the mat at the bottom – his stupid wife always polished the floors under the mat – picked himself up and shot into the lounge and behind the settee. His son quickly joined him but his wife ran about the room wailing 'Oh God, save us. Where are the deeds of the house, where are my rings?' I told her 'Get in with your family. If you survive, that is the time to sort things out!' After this first experience the family brought in railway sleepers and stacked them up against the outside wall of the understairs cupboard to make an indoor air raid shelter.

There was another night air raid a week or two later. The family were all in their cubby hole under the stairs while I stayed in bed, thinking if I had to die then I might as well do it in comfort. Then I heard a stick of bombs coming our way and the last one landed in the field behind the house, my bed jumping up and down again with the blast. Downstairs, the dining room window had been blown in and slivers of glass like daggers were embedded in the opposite wall. The next morning we looked around outside; there was a bundle of pea sticks leaning against the garden shed and a piece of shrapnel had made a neat hole through the lot and through the shed to embed itself in the wall of the house. A pony in the neighbouring field had been badly hurt and a vet had to put it down. We had been very lucky, a phrase I was going to use many times in my life!

The Winter Gardens ballroom in Weston held regular dances throughout the war, air raids permitting. About six of us went when we could and made friendships with some local girls. One night a professional couple gave a demonstration dance, and we stood behind the girls enjoying the display. One of the chaps was a cook back at the camp; he stood close to his girlfriend, took her hand and brought it back behind her to slip a raw sausage into it! She screamed enough to raise the roof, and everybody stopped and glared at us in horror.

One Saturday I woke up feeling really groggy, but I had been picked to play in the 1st 15 rugby team at Filton, Bristol. I struggled through the match feeling like nothing on earth, praying that the ball wouldn't come my way. On the Sunday morning I couldn't get out of bed and I was so ill my two mates had to help me to the sick quarters, where I was diagnosed with pleurisy. After a course of awful M & B tablets I recovered but the medical officer wouldn't discharge me until I had two wool vests. Len Huck went to town and bought me a couple but I soon gave up wearing them as they irritated my skin like mad. I packed them and posted them to my grandfather.

970 Squadron – RAF Barrow-in-Furness

Around this time [probably in early spring, 1941] I was posted back to RAF Cardington to join 970 Squadron. I arrived at the main gate, showed my papers and was told by the orderly sergeant that there was no such squadron at Cardington! He sent for the orderly officer and I thought they suspected that I was a spy. The officer went off to ring the CO, and came back full of apologies. Apparently there was a new barrage balloon squadron being formed and I was there to start organising things. I was shown to some empty billets by the square where I lived alone for a week until I finally received instructions. People began to arrive and I sorted them by trades – cooks and butchers in one hut, motor engineers and transport in another, barrage balloon riggers in a third and so on. Finally the senior officers arrived and I could take things a bit more easily.

When the whole squadron was assembled we moved out to Barrow-in-Furness in Cumberland. We started in convoy which was all very well until we reached Manchester and its traffic lights.

Nobody knew where to go except the CO who was at the front. The lights split us up and chaos ensued. It was like Tom and Jerry, as sections of us took different roads until one turned and it then became Jerry chasing Tom! We finally all met up somewhere up in the Pennines. We eventually arrived at Barrow and I was stationed at the headquarters, a lovely old house in Abbey Road surrounded by its own grounds.

The balloon units were scattered all around; some were on Walney Island, and one balloon unit was stationed in a populated area in the town which was hardly ideal. The balloon site was quite windy; the balloons were fitted with stabilisers on the back which only worked when the balloon was fully inflated, keeping it into the wind. Strong gusts meant the balloon rose too early and on reaching the roof tops would start to thrash about like a fish on a hook, taking off chimney stacks and roof tiles alike. The residents were not best pleased.

The balloons were also prone to accidents. Sometimes a balloon would pick up static electricity and burst into flames without warning. In high winds the steel cables sometimes snapped; once a balloon rigger was climbing onto the winch truck and was balanced with one foot on the wheel and one on the bed of the truck, when the cable snapped and whipped down almost severing his thigh.

Some of the lads were living in a converted chicken shed out on Walney Island. They met a merchant seaman in a pub and he sold them a monkey that he had brought back from his last trip. All went well – although the monkey used to bite them a bit – until one night they gave it some brown ale whereupon it went berserk and attacked them. They had to evacuate the hut smartly and they spent half the night outside in the cold looking in the window at the monkey. In the end they coaxed it outside and all rushed in and shut the door. Next morning there was no sign of the monkey.

There were two of us sergeants at HQ and we had things running pretty well until one day a warrant officer arrived (he'd been promoted to WO as soon as he'd been called up because that had been his rank in the old Royal Flying Corps). There were the three of us in the sergeant's mess – the lounge of the original house – and this chap used to get on our nerves. He had been a salesman for Lyon's cakes before the war. He was going bald and was quite uptight about it. I persuaded him to try a certain cure that I had – a blend of paraffin and petroleum jelly – which he rubbed into his scalp each night. After several weeks he had to discontinue the 'treatment' as his wife complained of the smell!

By this time I was getting restless and wanted more action, so I volunteered for aircrew. After a series of medical and educational examinations [at RAF Padgate, near Warrington] I received notice to go down to London for further examinations and interviews. In October 1941, I joined others for a day of exams at the aircrew reception centre [ACRC] at Regents Park, opposite the zoo. The following day I was told that I had passed, and then had to attend medical examinations carried out by Harley Street specialists. These were very thorough physical exams and included tests for night vision and colour blindness. After two days of this we had an interview in front of six very senior officers- all pilots or navigators. They asked me why I wanted to be a pilot and what I would like to fly - fighters, bombers or internal transport. I told them I'd prefer fighters and after a short discussion the group captain said 'Well, sergeant, we think you'll make a very good fighter pilot. Good luck! '

I went back to my unit at Barrow, proudly wearing the white flash on my hat indicating that I had been selected for aircrew training.

Not long after this, a notice went up on the daily orders board asking for volunteers to go on a commando course. I went to see the adjutant to volunteer and he turned me down, as I was waiting to start the pilot's course. However, soon he was posted elsewhere and an inexperienced chap took over. I took the white flash off my hat and went up to volunteer again. This time it worked; he was delighted that someone had come forward.

So I was seconded to the King's Own Yorkshire Light Infantry Commando barracks at Formby, on the coast between Liverpool and Blackpool. The first week just about killed us but after that we got fit and started to enjoy it, or rather some of us did – others really struggled physically, especially on the assault course. We had to be on the square at 6.30am in PE kit for exercises. It was pitch dark so I used to stand at the back and wave my arms about a bit, it looked good in the shadows!

I didn't like the sergeant instructor much, he was always boasting how tough he was. One day we were learning how to take a 9mm anti-tank gun apart – a longish heavy gun with two legs which you sunk into the earth as you fired 9mm shells. He boasted that not many people could fire it from the shoulder, as he could. Well, I had to stand up for the RAF; I couldn't let the Army beat us. The recoil sent me back a step or two but I did it! That wiped the conceited smile off his face.

We used to go on night manoeuvres in a big wood. The instructors would wait in hiding and suddenly throw thunder-flashes at us. We soon got smart, after we came across a church hall where the WVS supplied tea and cakes; while the army were searching for us with their thunder-flashes and blank ammunition at the ready, we were having a cup of tea and a sit-down. We set a watchman outside to warn us, and after a couple of nights he shouted 'They're coming'. We beat a hasty retreat through a window at the back.

One of the exercises was a bit uncomfortable. The beach at Formby is very flat and when the tide is out you can walk for miles. One moonlit night we had to wade out and take tickets off posts which were set several hundred yards out. By the time we reached the posts the water was up to our chests. All the time the army was firing live rounds and the bullets were hitting the water about ten to 15 yards from us and ricocheting away.

We were taught how to arm hand grenades with detonators, then from a trench throw them over a length of chicken wire stretched between two poles about 20ft high. One clumsy idiot managed to let one slip out of his hand as he was throwing, and it landed just behind our trench. We all leapt out like arrows from a bow, as there was a seven-second delay before the grenade exploded.

RAF Regent's Park & RAF Brighton

Finally word came for me to report to start my pilot's course at ACRC, St Johns Wood, London. On arrival I was accommodated in a luxury flat with two others, in Viceroy Court, Regents Park; we had the top righthand flat at the front. We could lie in bed and listen to all the jungle noises from the zoo just across the way.

At first I stuck out a bit because I was already a sergeant and the others were all newly joined-up but we soon forgot the difference in rank and we treated each other as equals. The only time that rank made a difference was when we had to march anywhere, like marching to Lord's cricket ground every Friday for pay parade, and then as a sergeant I was in charge. While waiting at Lords we often had time to have a bat at the nets so I can honestly say I have played cricket at Lords.

On one occasion I had to march them a fair way through London to a theatre, where they were making a recording to send out to our troops abroad. The same thing happened with traffic lights as occurred in Manchester but the leading bunch that got through had the intelligence to halt and mark time until the lights changed and the second bunch caught up.

I left the chaps in a yard at the back of the theatre while I went to find out what we had to do. As I stood at the door, a very attractive young lady came up and asked 'How do you get into this place?' I indicated the door. Later, when the show was underway, she came on stage and I realised she was Pat Kirkwood, a well-known star in those days. Our task in the show was to be the audience and respond when a chap held up a board carrying instructions – laugh, clap, whistle, stop, etc.

While I was at St Johns Wood a parcel arrived from my mother. It had been sent to Barrow-in-Furness, then on to somewhere else, and finally reached me after about a month. In the parcel were a number of things including a bacon-and-egg pie, now covered in mould! I took the pie over to the zoo and threw bits to the bears. Later on, one of my mates tried to convince me they were looking for the chap who had poisoned the bears.

During our time at the centre we had a stream of medical tests and lectures on things such as maths and meteorology. As part of my medical examinations, I had all my recent tooth fillings drilled out, and replaced with stuff that wouldn't fall out at high altitudes. Some mornings we went to the Seymour Baths where we had to practise the emergency 'ditching' procedure. We had to strip and dress in old uniforms and flying boots, get into a dinghy, turn it over deliberately, then turn it upright and climb aboard. When we had completed all the training to their satisfaction we were moved to Brighton.

The RAF had requisitioned the Grand Hotel and the adjoining Hotel Metropole [in October 1941]. I was in the Grand on the second floor at the front (this was the site of the 1984 IRA bombing during the Tory Party conference, when Margaret Thatcher was PM). The Grand Hotel might have been the height of luxury in peacetime but in 1940 it had been stripped of everything for our occupation. There were no carpets and the bare boards had large gaps between them; the floors sloped so much to one side that anything round that was dropped would roll across the room. We slept in RAF beds and had steel lockers for our gear.

The whole beach at Brighton had been barb-wired and mined in preparation for a German invasion. Every now and then a shout of 'Dog, dog!' would sound all over the hotel, and everybody would rush to the windows to see a dog running along the beach until 'Wumph!' and bits of dog flew high and wide. The army were in charge of the beach and they knew where the paths were through the minefield, so by arrangement they would escort us down to have a swim over by Black Rock.

4

LEARNING TO FLY
1942

We left Brighton in spring, 1942, and moved to Newquay where we were stationed in the Edgecliff Hotel. I shared a room with another sergeant who was a bit weird; he was a yoga fanatic and would spend hours sitting cross-legged staring at the wall. One evening I was sitting on my bed reading a book while he was meditating, and suddenly he toppled over in a dead faint or trance. It took quite a while for him to come out of it.

The Edgecliff was ideal for us. We could go down the steps to the beach each evening for a swim, come back up and hop into a hot bath. We were there from May to September! The whole of Newquay was taken over by the RAF. Most of the hotels were requisitioned and full of aircrew trainees; the streets were empty except for delivery traffic so every morning we drilled in the street. We spent a lot of time studying navigation, aerodynamics, meteorology and even camp sanitation.

Many of us were likely to get commissions so all these skills would come in handy if we were captured or left in charge of other aircrew. I was offered a commission to the rank of flying officer but I turned it down when I realised that the officers' mess fees would cancel out the pay rise. Besides, I was happier messing with the men (had I known I was destined to end up as a POW I would have benefitted by getting a higher allowance, and officers also received camp money known as *lager geld*).

Some weekends I would cycle over to St Columb to see my

aunt, uncle and cousins Jean, Mary and John (who, by the way, could trace their family further back than the time of Elizabeth I; unfortunately the line died out with my uncles and cousins, who left no heirs or had daughters who didn't continue the family name). Uncle Stan was friendly with the landlord of the *Red Lion*. A gang of us used to cycle over there and dance with local girls in one of the spare rooms. I remember that the road surface was poor and I got endless punctures and often found myself walking for miles. Despite all the fit young men in Newquay in those days, there was rarely any trouble, unlike today when undisciplined yobs descend upon the town in the summer.

After I passed out from the initial training wing at Newquay, I was posted to the flying training wing at RAF Desford, near Leicester. It was here that I at last learnt to fly. We were trained in de Havilland Tiger Moths, a 1930s single-engine bi-plane. My instructor was a sergeant like me and we got on pretty well. He was quite mad at times; we would fly out over the countryside and make for an isolated cottage where his girlfriend lived, and he would 'buzz' her by suddenly dropping, zooming over the roof, narrowly missing the chimney pots.

We spent a lot of time doing 'circuits and bumps' – taking off, landing, taking off again, doing a circuit and then landing again. I preferred to have my safety straps loose so that I could lean over the side to see how far I was off the runway. One morning we set off to do circuits and bumps as usual, with my instructor at the controls. 'It's a beautiful day. Let's go up and play around a bit' he said. When we got up to about 7000ft he took the plane into a few sweeping loops and stalls, then suddenly turned it upside down. My straps were loose and I thought I was about to fall out! I made a grab for the dashboard, gashing my hand, and there I was dangling out of the cockpit! The instructor found it very amusing.

After just seven hours of accompanied instruction he reckoned I was ready to fly solo. What a nasty feeling it was to be up there all by myself for the first time, with no one to take over if things went wrong! One of my mates was up on his first solo and we watched him land. We could guess what he was thinking by the sound of his engine. It was a case of 'No, I can't, I'll over-shoot. Yes I can… no, I can't!'. By now he was well along the runway and decided he couldn't land in time, so he gave her a burst and got just enough airspeed to rise and belly-flop on top of a hangar. The hangar was leased to Bolton & Paul, aircraft manufacturers, and luckily it was about 6pm and most of the workers had gone home. No-one was hurt, but there was a wrecked aircraft and a big dent in the roof. The pilot crawled to the edge of the roof and yelled for a ladder.

The instructors often joked that there was a guardian angel who looked after us trainee pilots; after a crash an aircraft would be just a heap of metal and nuts and bolts, then there would be a sudden upheaval in the middle and the trainee would appear casually dusting himself off!

I had my final flying test with the chief flying instructor, and I did pretty well. I remember that there was a cement factory with a plume of smoke rising from the chimney directly behind us on the ground. I had to turn the aircraft without side-slipping and finish with the nose directly in line with the factory, which I did, bang on. We were not told if we had passed. Instead we were sent to a dispersal centre in Heaton Park, Manchester, where we lived in a battery of Nissen huts for a few days. Then we were assembled in front of a huge building – about two hundred of us from various flying training schools. The adjutant came out onto a balcony and confirmed what we had already suspected from the rumours that we heard: there was a bottleneck of pilots and we would have to re-train as navigators or bomb-aimers (air bombers as they were officially known) or go straight to an operational squadron as gunners. We were dismayed that almost two years had been wasted, and there was almost a riot; a lot of foot-stamping and calls for the CO to come out and face us. I didn't fancy sitting in a gun turret nor could I face another six months' training as a navigator, so I opted for a four-month course to become an air bomber in Bomber Command.

While waiting for a posting from Heaton Park we amused ourselves by getting up to mischief. The Nissen huts ran along an avenue of trees and the branches hung over the hut roofs – I suppose it helped camouflage them from air attack. A couple of chaps from our hut climbed a tree beside the neighbouring hut and jumped down from an overhanging branch onto the roof, knowing that everyone was out. Next they carefully dropped a thin glass bottle of lighter fuel down the chimney. When our neighbours returned later that evening, cold and wet, the first thing they did was light the stove. We heard a hell of a boom and they all came running out, wondering what had happened. They soon realised that we were the culprits and they got their own back a couple of nights later. We lit our stove one evening and the hut slowly filled up with dense smoke, and we had to evacuate the hut coughing and spluttering. Our neighbours had got on our roof and bunged up the flue with turf.

As usual I had to drill my fellow trainees in the squad. I was about to start drilling a new group when one of them came over and said 'Sarge, I believe you used to know a chap called Eddie Hooper – well, I was the runner for his father's bookie'. Eddie Hooper had been one of my best mates on my first posting to Cardington. He was a professional boxer from Liverpool who fought under the name of Edgar Snow, and his father was a bookmaker. This bookie's runner was a typical Liverpudlian 'wide boy'. One day we were drilling with sten guns – sub-machine guns which could easily be taken to bits – and as they drilled in front of me I noticed the squad were all carrying their rifles except him. When I asked where his rifle was, he began to pull various bits out from the pockets in his battledress and explained 'Er, sarge, it's easier to carry it this way.'

RAF Millom

When we eventually left Heaton Park for our various courses, the majority of the chaps were sent to America or Canada to do the rest of their training, while I was sent to RAF Millom in Cumberland, because, as a sergeant, my rate of pay would be too expensive when converted to dollars. Millom was about two miles from camp and the most dreary, depressing place I had ever encountered.

We did our bombing practice in Avro Anson aircraft; I sat in the righthand seat and the pilot and I would take it in turns to wind up the undercarriage by hand; this made us sweat like mad and then get freezing cold when we got up to height. We used 11½-pound practice bombs; in daylight they gave off smoke but at night we loaded ones which flared. One night I missed the target and instead hit the main fusebox on the bombing range – there was a flash and all the lights on the range went out. We were all called back to base and when I got back to the mess it was drinks from everyone as I was the hero of the day for curtailing the night exercises.

Not long before Christmas [1942], we'd been down to a pub in the village, and on the way back to the station we passed through a farmyard where we saw a lonely goose. We caught it and one chap wrapped the goose in his tunic, pushed its head up the sleeve, and put it back on under his greatcoat. We managed to get past the guardroom and hide the goose in the toilet at the end of the hut. We painted three stripes on his neck, called him Sergeant Goose, and fed him on scraps saved from our meals or stuff pinched from the cookhouse bins. About two days before Christmas the CO announced that if the goose wasn't returned to the farm he'd cancel all festive activities. So it was goodbye to Sergeant Goose.

Early on Christmas morning our door burst open while we were still asleep after a boozy time the night before. A dozen or so WAAFs charged in and tipped us out of bed on to the floor. Most of the men slept naked but I still had my pants on, so as I hit the floor I jumped up and made for the shower. Three girls were chasing me; I grabbed the first and dragged her under the shower and turned it on. She was in full uniform and got soaked. When I turned on the other two they fled screaming. Back in the hut it was bedlam and chaos all rolled into one, with beds upset, bedding and equipment all over the place and couples wrestling on the floor. I stood watching helpless with laughter knowing I was safe as none of the girls fancied a ducking. As soon as we had dressed and sorted out the mess we went to the WAAF quarters where we found the sergeant still in bed asleep. She obviously was not in on the raid, but we carried her and her bunk down to a camp crossroads and left her there.

The WAAF sergeant in charge of the cooks was a tough girl from Liverpool, and I used to get on with her alright, pulling her leg quite a bit. At Xmas dinner we were served by the officers, as was traditional, and I had enjoyed a really huge main meal but didn't have room for steamed pudding – at least that's what I thought. The WAAF sergeant had other ideas: 'You'll eat my Christmas pudding if it kills you!' she roared, and the cooks held me down while she shovelled spoon after spoon of pudding and custard into me.

I wasn't very keen on flying in the Boulton Paul Defiant fighter planes, which we used for machine-gunning practice; they were flimsy and seemed to be kept airborne by brute force and ignorance.

The gun turret was up on top of the fuselage and looked down on the pilot's cockpit. We would follow an aircraft towing a target drogue, and when I swung my turret round to track the target it felt as though my back was out in the thin air, a horrible sensation.

Towards the end of our course ten bomb-aimers arrived from training in Canada. Our bomb release mechanism was slightly different to theirs: the bomb was released when you pressed the 'tit' and a light came on to tell you the next bomb station was primed and ready to go. The aircraft they trained on in Canada showed a light only when there was a 'hang up' and the bomb had *not* gone. On his first bombing practise run, the Canadian-trained pilot pressed the tit to release the bomb and as the light came on he kept on pressing it, releasing bomb after bomb. Luckily the result was not too disastrous – a demolished garden shed and a flock of sheep scattered with only one killed. The chief bombing officer was furious and ordered them to have more training.

My final bombing exercise was cancelled owing to a mishap. Ours was the last of four bombers taxi-ing around the perimeter, and my pilot got too close to the Defiant in front and the propeller chewed into its tail-plane.

My mates at Millom were a good bunch of chaps and we had fun despite our depressing surroundings. Whist playing rugby I was kicked on the knee which cracked the kneecap, and when I came out of hospital I crept about on a stick, until the gang decided I should go down to the village with them. They pinched an 'acc' trolley – a flat-bed two-wheeled trolley used for carrying accumulators out to the aircraft to start them up – and pushed me down to Millom. Coming back after they'd had a few was a different matter, when they let the trolley go and I sailed down a sloping field to hit the hedge at the bottom.

One afternoon we reported for flying after lunch and three of us were told we had to fly to the airfield at Weston-super-Mare, just the pilots and bomb-aimers. Part of our training as bomb-aimers included detailed map reading. The Ansons were going to Weston for modification and were stripped of all navigation and wireless equipment, so we needed to map-read our course all the way. We had to land at Weston Zoyland first, and get in touch with air command at Weston so they could lower their barrage balloons for us to land. When we finally arrived we were told to stay at nearby RAF Locking until our aircraft were ready to return to Millom. This suited me as a lot of my old pals were still there and most of them had been promoted to senior posts. I had a whale of a time; the warrant officer in charge of the cookhouse remembered that I liked curry so it was on the menu the first day. We went down to Weston that evening for a pint but the yarn went around that we had been shot down, and no matter what we said to the contrary, people insisted in buying us drinks. We finished the night at our favourite chippy, known as Coffins.

25. The new recruit, October 1938

26. Drilling at RAF Cardington

27. Back home on leave

28. Bill with his mother, Flo (left) and Audrey

29. Bill with sister Una, 1939

30. Corporal William Warren, 1939

31. Posing on Len Huck's motorbike, RAF Locking

32. *Airmen training with the No 1 balloon unit at RAF Cardington, October 1940. In early 1941 Bill was tasked with the job of assembling the aircrews for the new 970 balloon squadron at Cardington, which then moved to its base at Barrow-in-Furness, Cumberland.*

33. *In October 1941, Bill passed his aircrew medical examinations and interviews at ACRC, Regents Park. He returned to 970 Squadron, now sporting the distinctive white flash on his cap, and waited to begin his pilot's training course.*

34. Bill's first flights as a trainee pilot were in a De Havilland Tiger Moth bi-plane at RAF Desford, in 1942. After switching to Bomber Command, he then trained at RAF Millom, first in Avro-Ansons (35, below left) and then in Boulton Paul Defiant fighters, (36, below right).

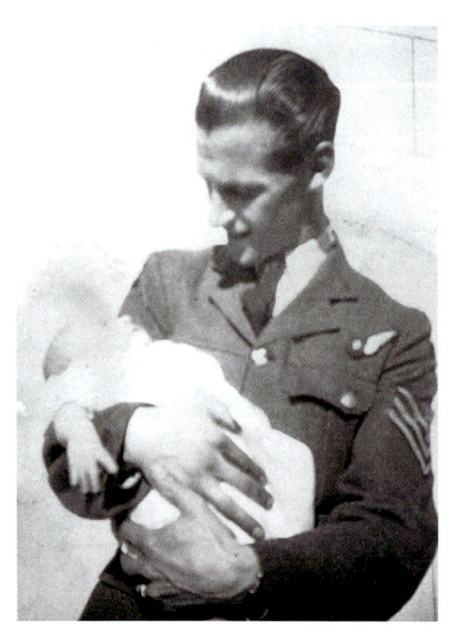

37 & 38. Bill home on leave, with his baby daughter Sandra, mother Flo and Granny Whiting

39. In early 1943, at RAF Edgehill, Bill and his now regular fellow aircrew trained in Vickers Wellington bombers, or 'Wimpys' (40 & 41, pictured right) before being posted to 1651 Heavy Conversion Unit at RAF Waterbeach.

42. A Wellington bomber of 214 Squadron at RAF Stradishall, Suffolk, undergoing repairs after damage sustained on bombing operations. Bill joined 214 Squadron around late spring, 1943.

43. Sections 3 and 4 of 214 Squadron, probably at Chedburgh, 1943. Bill and his fellow aircrew are in the second row. From left to right: navigator FS Ted Bamsey; bomb-aimer Sgt Bill Warren; wireless operator Sgt Joe Musgrove; pilot FS Ces Brown; and rear-gunner Sgt Tommy Brennan (not pictured are engineer Sgt Jock Harvey and mid-upper-gunner Sgt Bob Bentley).

44. Three Short Stirling bombers of 1651 Heavy Conversion Unit flying above RAF Waterbeach.

45. The Short Stirling was the RAF's biggest, heaviest bomber in World War II. Stirlings flew 14,500 sorties with Bomber Command; 582 aircraft were lost in action and 119 written off.

46. Pilot and co-pilot in the Stirling's cockpit.

47. The bomb-aimer (Bill's role) would lie prone in the nose of the aircraft, beneath the flight deck, peering down through the bomb sight.

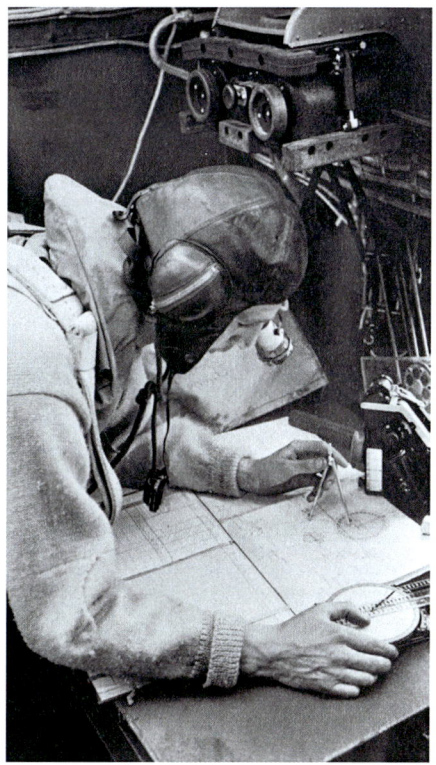

48. The navigator would plot the aircraft's course at his station located immediately behind the pilots' seats in the cockpit.

49. A Stirling bomber of 1651 HCU at RAF Waterbeach loads up with bombs prior to a mission.

50. A bomb-aimers view of a night raid over Hamburg in July 1943.
A photo-flash bomb (lower left) illuminates the town's lakes.

51. A cartoon of a night raid from Bill Warren's POW Wartime Log.

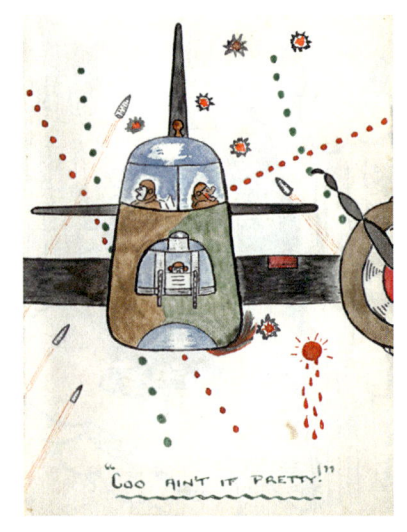

5

TAKING-OFF
1943

When we at last passed out at Millom we were sent to RAF Waterbeach in Cambridgeshire, put into a large room and told to form crews. There were ten pilots, ten navigators, ten bomb-aimers, ten wireless operators, ten flight engineers and 20 gunners. After a great deal of chopping, changing and swapping we sorted ourselves out. Our pilot was Cecil 'Ces' Brown, a football fanatic whose father was manager of Chester FC and had been manager of Torquay Athletic. Ces was a good bloke but after a while he began to have trouble with his eyesight, especially flying in poor light, so I often had to talk him down or take over the aircraft on night landings (oddly, when he finally found time to arrange an eye test we got shot down). I got on well with our navigator Ted Bamsey, his father owned a butcher's shop in Bath, and we always went to town together. His favourite expression was 'Couldn't I eat a plate of chitterlings right now!' The wireless operator was Joe Musgrove, he'd worked in Rowntree's chocolate factory in York. As bomb-aimer I completed the working part of the crew, as the gunners weren't involved in the flying of the aircraft. When all the crews were sorted we were told to leave our flying kit and uniforms and were sent on two weeks leave.

Travelling from Cambridge home to South Devon in those days was quite an adventure. I travelled light with a haversack, which was just as well as I arrived at Totnes in time to miss the last connecting train to Kingsbridge. It was a warm moonlit night and although there was no chance of a lift (roads were deserted after 10pm in wartime) I decided to walk the 12 miles. After about four miles I came across a friendly carthorse looking out over a gate. I stroked him for a bit then unlatched the gate, climbed up onto his back and using his thick mane to steer him, set off along the road riding bareback. He carried me all the way to the outskirts of Kingsbridge where I found a grassy field to shut him in for a well-earned rest and feed. I often wondered what the owners thought when they tracked him down to a field eight miles away!

On a different occasion when going on leave I again missed the last connection at Totnes but as it was a wet, rough night I laid up on the waiting room table with my kitbag for a pillow. A naval officer with a torch discovered me and seemed concerned that I was going to sleep there. He gave me a cigarette and left, returning a while later to say his host had invited me to stay for the night. I found myself at a big house above the town owned by Captain Liddell-Hart, a well-known writer of military books (the house later became the boarding house for King Edward Grammar School). I sat with them for a supper of chicken soup, cheese, biscuits and wine. Next morning the maid brought me a cup of tea in bed and ran a bath, and after breakfast the officer drove me down to the station to catch the first train to Kingsbridge.

RAF Edgehill

On our return from leave we were posted as a crew to RAF Edgehill, near Banbury, for further operational training. Before our first flight we went out to the aircraft to teach each other a bit about our jobs so that if anyone got hit by flak, the others could cover in an emergency. Joe, the wireless operator, didn't seem very clear about his tasks so we weren't brimming over with confidence when we started flying together on Wellington bombers [nicknamed 'Wimpys' after the portly character in the Popeye cartoons]. As bomb-aimer I spent hours in a special link trainer, lying on my stomach looking down at a projected countryside moving towards me at various speeds and light intensities. With a bomb tit in my hand, I had to steer the aircraft to the designated target and release the imaginary bombs.

We had to fly on all sorts of exercises, day and night. What I didn't like about Wimpys was that the petrol cocks were located over the main spar and some of them dripped onto the fabric-covered fuselage. In fact, on one night exercise, our Wimpy wasn't answering the throttles very well and on our return we found petrol pouring from one of the air intakes.

One night we finished our exercise at about 1am, climbed out and left the aircraft for the next crew who were waiting to do the same exercise. Joe realised he had left his parachute on board, but the other crew said they would hand it in when they returned (losing a 'chute was serious as we had to have them by us at all times). As we walked down the lane to the mess we stopped to watch the other crew taking off. The plane reached about 100ft then burst into flames. The guns started firing, set off by the heat, and then the aircraft crashed. The crew were all killed. We had noticed that some of them were smoking when they climbed aboard, and maybe they had set the petrol fumes alight.

On another occasion we had to fly a high ranking officer to Northern Ireland. As we crossed over Wales we flew into dense cloud, and trying to climb above it, we pulled up into very violent cumulonimbus storm clouds. A strong up-current lifted the nose of the aircraft steeply and we both pushed with all our strength on our joysticks. Nothing happened. Then the up-current abruptly died, leaving us hanging in the air, and both engines stalled. There was a deathly silence, and then we started diving. As we came out of the low cloud and saw the Welsh hills rushing up towards us I could only think what would be said in the mess the next day – 'Another crew gone for a Burton'. At the last minute the engines spluttered into life and we both hauled on our sticks to bring her out of the dive just in time. The officer was terrified – 'That's it, turn around and go back!' – and the navigator came on the intercom: 'Will you two b-----s stop messing about?'. When he emerged from his cubby hole and saw our white faces, he realised that we weren't playing. His 'Very' cartridges were all over the place as were all his maps and instruments (Very cartridges were flares of different colours used in emergency if we were fired upon by our own anti-aircraft guns; the colour combinations changed every four hours to ensure the enemy could not copy them and approach undetected, and all ship's captains, army commanders and pilots had lists of times and colours known as the 'colours of the day').

Edgehill airfield was stuck up on top of a hill, and sometimes when landing in the early morning we could only see the airfield strip as the surrounding valley was lost in mist; it was like landing on an aircraft carrier or a magic carpet.

Over a period of several weeks our crew were supposed to complete a series of star-and-moon shots using a sextant. We had to do about fifty readings outside in the cold and dark resting the sextant on an air raid shelter. It didn't take long for us to realise that we could use calculations to cook the results whilst sitting on our beds in the warmth of the hut. When the results were handed in no-one noticed that they were cooked.

One night an Irish mate borrowed a bike from a WAAF to take the two of us down the hill to the village pub two miles away. I sat on the handlebars, and as we descended the steepest bit of the hill there was a loud crack and we suddenly picked up more speed.

My mate shouted 'No brakes - jump!' just as we hit the hedge. We picked ourselves up as we started to walk on down the hill, my mate began to laugh so much he was unable to speak. It was then I noticed a coolness behind and found the seat of my trousers had been ripped out. So I had to go back for another pair of trousers.

1651 HCU – RAF Waterbeach

When we completed our advanced flying training we returned to Waterbeach, Cambridgeshire, to train on heavy four-engined aircraft [with the 1651 Heavy Conversion Unit – HCU]. It was just our luck that we were going to train on Short Stirlings, the biggest aircraft flying in the war at that time. They were well-made and could be thrown around the sky like a fighter plane, but were swines at take-off. Fully-loaded with fuel and eight tons of bombs, the aircraft would be difficult to control as she moved up the runway, swinging from side to side as the two pilots tried to get up sufficient speed for lift-off. The torque from the four propellers was all directed at the starboard wing, which didn't help. Bomb-aimers like myself, who had also trained as pilots, were always sent to Stirling squadrons as the plane needed two pilots opening and closing the throttles to control the swing at take-off. Civilians working out on the aerodrome frequently had to drop their tools and run for their lives, as sometimes the aircraft would veer 50 or 60 yards either side of the runway.

Stirlings were known to be death-traps due to their inability to gain height, and sometimes they didn't even make it off the ground. Apparently, during the design process, the air ministry boffins told Short Bros to reduce the wing span to less than 100ft to fit into the existing hangars. The margin between wingspan and lift was minimal, and the maximum height when loaded was 12,000ft – an easy target for flak. Any higher than this and the plane would start to wallow and yaw like a tired whale. Indeed, Air Vice-Marshall Harris once told Winston Churchill that he wanted Stirlings to be taken out of service, so many had been lost.

Whilst training at Waterbeach we had to carry out exercises known as 'bullseyes', flying to the Isle of Man, on up to Ailsa Craig, across to Flamborough Head and back again to base. Throughout the trip fighter planes would carry out mock attacks and we would have to take evasive action. After several hours spent throwing around a heavy bomber we would be so exhausted and fed-up that we ignored the attacking fighters. When they flew alongside to see what was up, we gave them two fingers.

We used to mess around a lot on long and boring exercises. Back aft was an Elsan toilet, and when one of the crew went to use it we would swing the plane around to fling them off the seat. One second they would be pinned to the floor, and then next up on the ceiling. To relieve the monotony Joe Musgrove would take out the radio coils connecting us to base and replace them with K-coils which enabled us to get the BBC and listen to *Music While You Work*. On our return we were questioned as to why we hadn't answered the radio, and we blamed radio malfunction, although the technicians rarely found anything wrong.

One night we had to take an army officer and two sergeants up to show them what the blackout was like from the air. When we had got through take-off and struggled to make full height, the officer – a complete 'Blimp' – seemed quite scared, and I winked at the two sergeants. Soon we were in icing conditions, with blocks of ice dropping off the propellers and hitting the fuselage with terrific bangs. I looked worriedly over at the officer and pretended to reach for my 'chute, whereupon he grabbed his and put it on in a flash, to the quiet amusement of the sergeants.

214 Squadron FMS – RAF Chedburgh

Finally we were posted to 214 Squadron FMS, at Chedburgh, a satellite of RAF Stradishall near Bury St Edmunds in Suffolk (FMS stands for Federal Malay States, who sponsored the squadron, this was quite common during the war). Here we were assigned our aircraft, a Stirling Mk III, EF402 BU-E (BU identified the squadron, while E was our individual aircraft ID).

Life on the ground was much more relaxed on an operational squadron than we had been used to before. Our sleeping quarters were in a little valley away from the camp where we could sleep during the day without being disturbed. There were only two crews in the hut, the others were Australians. At lunchtime we would line up for the CO and the medical orderlies to give us a dose of Haliborange to prevent us getting colds; it had a fishy taste and repeated on us all day.

From the base we used to go to a pub called the *Cherry Tree* which was just a little way across the fields but miles by road. I often ended up half-carrying Jock Harvey, our Scottish flight engineer, as he didn't know when to stop drinking – luckily he wasn't very big. We had to cross a deep dry drainage ditch, and one night I climbed up the other side only to find he had fallen back into it. Back down again I went and managed to get him to the edge but by the time I had dropped down the other side he had disappeared again. The rest of the gang found it all very amusing.

Ted our navigator was always on about how he liked crab apples and the jelly his Mum used to make with them, so one night when he got very drunk we put him to bed and went back across the fields and broke a large branch off a crab apple tree and carefully draped it over him; when he woke up he thought he had ditched into a tree. We used to drink a lot when we weren't flying, because it helped us to forget about the next night. We reckoned that the people who lost their nerve were mostly teetotallers; when we had a night off, due to bad weather, they would go on worrying about it, while we would have a few pints and forget it until next morning, when there were other things to think about.

If we had been flying the night before, the tannoy in our hut didn't come on until midday. Then we were driven out to our aircraft to take off and check that all systems were OK, then land and taxi it up to the dispersal point where the armourers would 'bomb up' ready for that night's take-off. We always tried to get our air test done early and be first in the line-up for take-off that night. If we were first off, we could take time to gain height by circling the airfield, so that when the order came to 'set course' we were already up to height, whereas the last ones to take off often had to climb 'on track' which meant they had less time to gain height with their overload of bombs. No-one wanted to be 'tail end Charlie' as stragglers were often picked off by enemy night fighters.

After the air test I had to supervise the armourers to ensure the right bombs were on the correct station. Once this was done we went for lunch. We were given special food as some things – like beans – couldn't be digested at high altitude due to lack of air pressure outside the aircraft. The gases produced would swell up in our stomach abnormally. We could have as much milk as we liked, although milk was rationed. After lunch we went to the briefing room to learn about the target that night, and be given our course, expected weather conditions, cloud cover, wind direction and speed, land marks etc. The briefings were meant to be top secret, but in fact you could discover the target by listening to the gossip in the pub or village post office!

Briefing over, we were free to rest or do what we liked until dinner in the evening, then it was time to get into our flying suits, emptying the pockets of anything – even a bus ticket – which could give the Germans vital information should we be unfortunate enough to be captured. It was important to keep still as we waited for buses to take us out to the aircraft as any sweat trapped in the suits would quickly chill when we gained altitude. Arriving at the dispersal point all the aircraft looked like massive elephants lined up on a circus parade. There could be as many as seven bombers ready for take-off, although mostly there were only three or four, as there wouldn't have been time to replace the aircraft lost on previous trips; we'd generally lose two, three or four planes a night. We would stand or sit around waiting for all to be ready to climb aboard. The ground crew would come out to see us off and WAAFs brought us things to take with us – a thermos of coffee (which nearly always got broken), a tin of orange juice, some chewing gum (which we couldn't eat because of our masks) and caffeine citrate, known as 'wakey-wakeys'.

It was while we were waiting that the butterflies would start to flutter in our stomachs. I would wonder why I was stupid enough to volunteer for aircrew, and I would have given anything to be one of the ground staff at those moments. At a given signal we'd climb aboard and from then there was no time to be scared. We had about 30 pre-flight checks to complete. When the engines were started up and all the instruments had been checked, I would go down to the bombing platform to check my bomb sight and camera, then go aft and see to the photo flashes (45lbs of magnesium). At a certain time on our synchronised watches we'd taxi forward to the end of the runway and wait for a 'green' from the control caravan. We would run forward a bit to straighten up the tail wheel, then it was in the lap of the Gods as to what sort of take-off we would make. As we gained a bit of height we could see aircraft taking off in the twilight from other bases – Maidenhall, Lakenheath, Downham Market and Oakington. Often we'd see one burst into flames; we were all dangerously overloaded by as much as 1,000lbs, and would often struggle to get our plane to climb above the treetops. Once we had reached height, we would set off for the rallying point over King's Lynn and the Wash, where there would be hundreds of aircraft circling, and at the given time we would head out across the North Sea, the gunners testing their weapons by firing them down into the waves.

Sometimes we would load up with sea mines, and have to drop them on a 'G fix' off the Frisian Islands. On one occasion the Germans were able to jam the fix at 3 degrees east and although we could have dropped the mines using dead reckoning we had strict instructions not to, so instead we dropped two safely into the North Sea (where the Navy could recover them) and brought two back (this was necessary to bring us down with a safe landing weight). On landing, we taxied to our dispersal point where the aircrew bus arrived to take us back to camp, but as bomb-aimer I was responsible for the mines and had to wait until the armourers arrived to take over. Some nights I'd be sheltering under the wing for nearly an hour before they came.

These mining trips were code-named 'Gardening' and one mission involved laying sea mines between two islands off La Rochelle in the south of France. As we flew across France we looked down to see torches flashing V for Victory. When we reached our target we had to descend over the Isle de Re at 1,400ft and at less than 140mph. At the briefing we had been assured that the island was undefended – wrong! We dropped our mines OK but as we turned back over the island the flak was intense and we were hit. We were losing fuel fast and by the time we had struggled back to the Channel it was clear that we could not make it back to base.

Our wireless operator signalled 'Mayday' and as we approached the coast a searchlight came up to meet us. We followed the beam until we were picked up by another, then another, until an airfield switched on its landing lights and we were able to land. We had landed at a Yankee aerodrome and they were amazed at the size of our Stirling bomber.

At this time we were carrying a highly secret device, (code-named H2S) which was able to identify man-made objects on the ground and also along the coastline, against the dark sea at night. We were the first main force squadron to carry H2S and while we were under instruction we were in a hut away from other buildings and surrounded by RAF police. On the plane it was housed in a big 'blister' underneath the fuselage. The screen was in the navigator's cabin on which he could pick out objects such as buildings, or ships at sea; the land showed up as light green and the sea as black, so it was ideal for following a coastline.

We stayed on the aerodrome for three days while the ground staff carried out repairs, living off the fat of the land – the Americans certainly didn't know anything about rationing! We covered up the H2S screen whenever we went for meals and always left one of the crew on guard, although the Americans were very good at respecting our secrecy.

On one of our night raids on Mannheim the enemy searchlights came up as usual, vertically like the bars of a circus cage, and we got through them and dropped our bombs. On our return we took the biggest dog-leg ever, right down around the south of France. Ted the navigator was a bit concerned about his plotting as there was no way of checking the wind speed or direction so he asked Joe the wireless op for a radio fix. Joe gave him what he described as a 'first class' fix, but Ted said 'if that fix is right we're right over the centre of Chunking!' and instead carried on regardless and brought us out over the French coast dead on target. We noticed that on this part of the coast there was only darkness, no flak or searchlights, so on future flights we would always make a detour to cross the coast at that point, if we were near enough. Later when, we were prisoners, we heard that this stretch of coast was where the Allies had landed in Normandy – we reckoned they had pinched our quiet corner!

Returning to base from Germany on another night, we were up in the stack, waiting for our turn to land, when all hell was let loose in the runway below. A Canadian pilot was just coming in to land when a German bomber flew down the runway from the opposite direction dropping bombs. The Canadian let out a string of expletives on the RT and we were told to switch off as there were WAAFs on duty who could hear it all through our connection to base. I could guess that we obviously wouldn't be able to land there and would have to be diverted. I suggested we climb higher and when we got our instructions to re-locate we would be ready to get nose down, pick up some speed and reach our new landing place first. We were diverted to our old training station at Waterbeach. On the way I said we had better make a good landing to show the trainees how the operational crews fly, but we were in such a hurry to land that we 'ballooned' two or three times like a bouncing ball.

Flying back from another raid, we hit thick fog approaching England so we were instructed to head for the westcountry and land wherever we could find a lit runway. We eventually found one and radioed for permission to land, but got no reply (Joe was probably on the wrong wavelength). We decided to land anyway as we were very low on fuel, but I did worry it might have been a dummy runway cluttered with concrete and junk to trap enemy aircraft desperate to land. We touched down safely and the airfield orderly officer got the cooks out of bed to make us breakfast (it was about three in the morning) and he then had to smash open a barrack room for us to 'crash out' – we were just about asleep on our feet. On waking I found a copy of the *Kingsbridge Gazette* under my bed! When we came to take off the next morning we had a bit of trouble as the runway was too short for our large Stirling bomber; we aborted the first attempt, but made it on the second.

We got a new CO called McGlynn [in July, 1943], who hadn't flown on many operations. During one briefing he told us that from now on we were not to weave but fly straight and level (we always veered a couple of miles either side of track to confuse the German radar). Afterwards we had a talk with the other crews and we all decided to carry on weaving, as before. The next morning they woke up our crew and told us to fly the CO's groundcrew to Coltishall (a fighter station) and bring back McGlynn and his aircrew as they had been badly shot up – so much for straight and level flying! Taking off from Chedburgh we made a bad lift and the groundcrew sergeant who was standing up holding on to our seats was heard to mumble that he'd never fly again. It was even worse when we came down at Coltishall as the fighter runway was much too short. We managed to drop down, brake like mad and stopped just short of the hedge at the end of the runway. We picked up McGlynn and his crew, and we asked if he wanted to fly her but he declined, so we got the Stirling's tail right against the boundary hedge and gave the engines all they would take and prayed. There were what looked like council houses at the far end of the field and I reckon we missed the chimney pots by inches.

Another of McGlynn's daft ideas was that aircrews were not fit enough and that we ought to go on cross-country runs instead of our favourite exercise of wine, women and smoking. The first time the bad weather prevented us flying, he had us on parade in our

PE kit and shoved us into two lorries to take us ten miles from the camp, for us to run back. The roads around the camp were narrow and twisty and each time the lorries slowed at a bend four or five of us dropped off the tailboard, until everyone was out. By the time the lorries had covered a mile they were empty and by the time they were ten miles away, we were all back in our huts lying on our beds, having a smoke!

McGlynn was livid so the next time he watched us loaded in to the lorries and then followed in his staff car. Now, one of my jobs was to map-read (for which I had trained) so I knew the lay of the land around the airfield; the road went around in a ten-mile arc but it was only about a mile directly across country. When the rest set off to run the ten miles back to base, a few of us headed across the fields once the CO had driven off. Soon we realised we were in park land, and looking back we saw a stag bearing down on us with evil intent! There was an iron fence in front of us which we cleared in double-quick time. Further on we were making our way through dense shrubs when we suddenly came upon a massive stately home (I later discovered we had made a detour through the Marquis of Bristol's estate). Eventually we crept into camp by the rear gate, well ahead of the rest of the squadron.

If we weren't flying at night the squadron had buses which took the aircrew to Cambridge or Bury St Edmunds. Ted and I usually opted for Cambridge, where our favourite pub was the *Barrel of Beef*. We got friendly with Lancaster and Halifax crews but after a while they started to avoid us. We eventually got it out of them that they considered it unlucky to get too close to Stirling aircrews as we carried an aura of death about us.

Sometimes Ted and I returned to camp on the aircrew bus, but occasionally we'd stay the night at the YMCA. One night we were walking through Cambridge when we found a £1 note on the pavement. We went into the nearest bar, put the note on the top and managed to get four Pimms each out of it, they were only half-a-crown each in those days. We ended up in the Polish YMCA that night, and halfway through the night I woke with a dose of the runs and found Ted was in the only toilet on the landing. We took it in turns sitting on the toilet for the rest of the night – some of the fruit in the Pimms must have been rotten.

At other times we'd go to Bury St Edmunds where I was friendly with a girl whose father was the landlord of a pub. After chucking-out time a few of us would be invited into the back room to listen to her Bing Crosby and Glenn Miller records. Her dad would usually bring in a bottle of whisky, which was in short supply during the war.

On one trip we were flying across the North Sea. The rear gunner, Tommy Brennan, reported a malfunction on two of his guns after testing them, and we were also having difficulty in getting higher than 7,000ft due to a temperature inversion (this occurs when a mass of hot air gets trapped above cold air,) because Stirlings had such a short wingspan. We couldn't get the lift and the plane just wallowed and yawed and was lifeless. The enemy searchlights on the Dutch coast were coming up in front of us so we decided to abort the mission. When we got back to base the CO played hell with us in the de-briefing room, until control reported that another returning aircraft was landing, and then another, including the squadron leader, so we were exonerated. It would have been suicide to have carried on at that height.

De-briefing followed every operation. We would give a detailed report of the flight including positions of searchlights, intensity of flak, success of bomb dispersal, wind and weather conditions and so on. We were given coffee and biscuits, and rum to empty our lungs of exhaust and petrol fumes (in reality to steady our nerves and cloud the memory of the night's experiences). Those who lost their nerve were a pitiful sight; they were taken off flying and put to work in the kitchens, their airforce records scrawled across with 'lack of moral fibre.' I remember a flight engineer from our hut who returned from a mission to Italy in tears, saying he didn't want to fly again. He had switched over the wrong fuel cocks and the engines had cut out over Mont Blanc. As the plane went into a dive he realised what he'd done and switched them back again. The next day he was washing pans in the kitchen – a warning to the rest of us.

Most operations followed a similar pattern to begin with. As we approached Holland we could see a line of searchlights stretching all along the Dutch coast, and behind this line was the 'fighter box' where the German fighter planes would be waiting. There were two types of fighters, which the Germans called 'wild boars' and 'tame boars'. The tame boars were guided by radar but the wild boars were free to fly as they thought fit. As we reached the coast the wireless op would release 'window' – thin strips of metal designed to throw up 'blips' on the enemy radar screens similar to those produced by aircraft, so that the anti-aircraft guns didn't know what to aim for. If we cleared the fighter box unscathed we started to look out for landmarks such as rivers, railway lines, lakes or bays like the Zuider Zee.

Sometimes it would be necessary to drop a flare for the rear gunner to aim his guns at, and then read off the degree of angle underneath his sights. This would enable the navigator to check the degree of drift, in case there had been a change in the predicted wind speed and direction.

As we flew on into Germany we might see a dummy target which the enemy had set up, hoping to fool us into wasting our bomb load, but they were usually lit with electric lights which burned too brightly, whereas marker incendiaries would have burned red and the edges of the 'stick' would be irregular. When we saw the real target looming up in the distance it was already well alight, marked by green indicator flares dropped by the pathfinders – pilots in Mosquitos or light-loaded Lancasters high above the danger zone. Now was the time for me to go down to the bombing platform and set up my bomb sight camera and photo-flashes. Everything was timed so that the camera took five pictures, the third one in the sequence timed to record the middle one of the stick of bombs or incendiaries, at the same time as the flash went off. Woe betide the bomb-aimer who came back with a picture of green fields in his camera!

During the approach to the target only the pilot and myself were allowed to speak on the intercom. I would get the target between the lines of my bomb sight and give corrections to Ces such as 'left... right... steady, steady' and then 'bombs going... bombs gone, bomb doors closed'. On one trip to Mannheim I couldn't find the target and gave the dreaded words 'Dummy run!' There was a long silence during which I could almost hear their prayers. It meant we had to pull out of the steady stream of bombers, fly back past them to re-enter the stream with the next wave of bombers, all in pitch darkness, all at near enough the same height and all blacked-out. The gunners would be screaming 'one 20ft above us,' or 'I can see into the engines of one behind us' or 'one just above to the left', and all the time we would be buffeted by the slipstream of the planes in front of us. On a second bombing run the pathfinders would have dropped more TIs (Target Indicators) and I would then be able to identify the target. Often, whilst approaching a target or even flying over it, we would see other bombers being shot down in flames and know that seven of our colleagues were being burnt alive on the way down. Sometimes as many as a dozen aircraft at a time would suffer this horrible fate, and we'd be thanking our lucky stars that it wasn't our turn.

The final mission

Our last operation was as part of a major assault on Hannover on the night of 27 – 28 September, 1943. I was 23 years old, and now a flight sergeant. We had been through the usual procedures on the ground and completed all the engine, instrument and bomb checks and were ready for take off, first in line as we usually tried to be. We took off at 20.13 and moved on track towards King's Lynn to circle and wait for the rest of the Stirlings to join us. The late evening sun was quite beautiful, the butterflies had almost left our stomachs, and now we had work to do and other things to think about. At the specified time each aircraft moved into position and we set course across the North Sea. We were well out to sea when Tommy the rear gunner shouted 'Junkers 88 coming up behind!'

The enemy opened fire so we had to do a double corkscrew to get him off our tail – the Stirling bomber was the only four-engine aircraft which would stand this kind of treatment. We put our Stirling into a steep dive to port, then the two of us pulled on the joysticks with all our strength to bring her out of the port dive and over into a starboard dive. We lost the Junkers but we were now down to 3,000ft. We slowly climbed back to height and carried on to the Dutch coast which by now was lined by searchlights side-by-side. If we got caught in a searchlight we would flash straight through it and out into the darkness; by the time the light had stopped its sweep and come back, we were long gone. But if we tried to fly away from the searchlights they would follow and pinpoint us until other lights joined in; this was known as 'coning' and almost always meant sudden death from the fighters.

As we ducked and dived to avoid the searchlights we also had to contend with masses of shells bursting all around us. As the tracers rushed up from the ground they seemed to be moving very slowly, until they got level and then we would realise just how fast they were travelling. Between each tracer shell there were six or seven others – invisible high explosive, shrapnel or armour-piercing shells – and all around there were aircraft exploding or going down in flames.

Leaving the searchlights behind we now had to run the gauntlet of the fighter box, and coming from the west, we were silhouetted against the lightest part of the sky. We were flying straight and level towards the target, Ted was in his corner with a dim light over his desk as he concentrated on keeping the course I was setting, while Ces watched for fighters and the approaching target.

We were late on the target due to the incident with the Junkers and most of the other bombers were already on their way home – at least, the ones who had survived. I released the bombs and closed the bomb doors, then leaned out and over to observe the fires and flashes and explosions, so I could make my report at de-briefing. I had just got back to my seat from the bomb platform when I saw a shell burst immediately ahead of us, then another even closer, then a third exploded underneath the fuselage. The plane shot upwards with the impact before we could control it, Ces and I both pushing our 'sticks like mad to bring her nose down again, but there was a terrific drag on the port wing and when I could shine a torch out of the window I saw that the port inner engine was a mass of twisted metal. We feathered the propeller to prevent it from causing a fire if it continued to turn, but from then on we had to take it in turns to fly her. We had to counteract a strong pull from the port wing, pressing down hard with our left foot and pushing up with our left arm, which was exhausting after just a few minutes. I became very hot and threw off my sheepskin flying jacket, leaving on my white crewneck pullover.

We were struggling to maintain height so we got Jock, our flight engineer, to chuck out the armour-plated doors, ammunition and anything else that was weighing us down. After an hour we were still not maintaining enough height to keep us out of range of the enemy guns, and the fuselage was getting peppered by flak, although nothing had yet hit our wing petrol tanks. Our remaining three engines were using too much fuel to keep height on high revs, and it was gradually becoming clear that we were not going to make it back to England.

Suddenly Bob Bentley, the mid-upper gunner, gave a shout that he'd been hit. Jock and Joe frantically climbed up the ladder to the gun turret, dropping down the hinged seat before they could reach him, but Bob was now semi-conscious. Between them they managed to lift him forward enough and fold back his seat so they could squeeze him down into the main fuselage. Bob had a severe wound in the back of his thigh which was bleeding profusely, and all three of them were drenched in blood; we realised that he would soon bleed to death. There was no time to tie a tourniquet on his thigh, but we made do with a bit of rope, and then pushed him out of the plane with a static line attached to his ripcord, so we could release his parachute when he was clear of the aircraft. We hoped his 'chute would get picked up by the searchlights and he might get rescued (we later heard that he was met by ground forces and taken to hospital right away, before finishing up in a prison camp).

Next we looked at our own chances of survival. Our first thoughts had been to ditch in the North Sea, but we were flying very low at 3,000ft, as straight as we could to get out to sea, and there was so much flak it was like weaving through a firework display. We were way off course, and Ted asked me if I could recognise any landmarks. I looked out and realised we were over the coast at Emden, where we'd been on a previous operation. We knew now that we couldn't get back to England, and anyway, the survival rates for getting out of a ditched Stirling at sea were very slim indeed. We were under close fire from below, holes were being punched all over the fuselage and a fire had started near the main spar. We all agreed to bale out. We were rather low to jump safely, so we pushed the throttles 'through the gate' (the thin wires across the throttle tops which were only to be used in an emergency) and this gave enough power to push us up to 7,000ft.

Ces gave the order 'abandon aircraft' and from there on everything went like clockwork, just as we had been trained. First we heard 'rear gunner jumping', as Tommy swung his turret around and went over backwards, then it was 'wireless operator jumping' and 'flight engineer jumping' as Joe and Jock leapt through the side door. I had to open a hatch in the bombing platform floor, which took me some time as it was stiff, but with a superhuman yank it suddenly jerked open. Ted was sitting on the bottom step waiting to go; I watched him put his feet out first and the slipstream nearly wrenched them off. When he had gone I sat on the bottom step, held my parachute tight under my left arm, clutched the ripcord in my right hand, and went through head first. As I jumped, what struck me most was the sudden silence, the deafening roar of the engines fading away as the plane continued on under automatic pilot into the darkness [it flew north for 500km before crashing near Galtho in Denmark, in farmer Jens Jensen's field].

I counted up to ten quickly and then pulled the ripcord. It came away in my hand, making me think I had broken it! I must have been falling head first and when the parachute opened I felt a bang over my right eye which started to bleed. Then there was a terrific agonising jerk between my legs, bringing me up the right way and pulling one of my flying boots off. I was now suspended in mid-air with shells bursting all around and searchlights trained on me. In the light and dark it seemed as if I would float for ever as a sitting target. After a while the guns stopped firing but I was still held in the searchlights, and I heard an enemy fighter plane approaching. We'd heard that the Germans had been shooting at parachutists, and the fighter came in close, before turning away; the pilot must have been checking to see if it was a man or a land mine.

After a long while, or so it seemed, the lights went out and I was descending slowly in total darkness. I reached down and held my foot to warm it up, but my 'chute started to swing so I corrected it by pulling on the correct cord. I decided that I would try to make for Holland when I got down, as we'd been told at escape briefings that if we reached a Dutch town or village there was a chance that a knock on the door might put us in touch with the Resistance. I was gazing up at the Plough and the Pole Star when my 'chute began to swing again and then I hit the ground with a thump, which knocked me out.

6

PRISONER OF WAR
1943

When I came round I untangled myself from the parachute and stamped it into the mud, as we had been instructed, then took another look at the stars and set off into the dark. It was pitch black, until I saw little lights in a line in front of me. I quickly changed direction and immediately ran into something which I think was a row of runner beans. I then started running towards the only gap in the line of lights that I could see, and fell over again having tripped over a row of cabbages.

By this time I had managed to kick off my other boot as it was causing me to be unbalanced, and I was going flat out when suddenly I went head first into a ditch or dyke, and the next thing I knew I was surrounded by German soldiers and two of them were picking me up. When they got me on my feet I could see a rifle on the ground by the light of their torches, and a third soldier grabbed the rifle and pointed it at me. I think they were young recruits as they seemed a bit tentative. I was marched across some fields, my back now aching from the parachute drop, until we finally reached a gun emplacement.

A young officer there could speak a bit of English; he was a rather keen type. Before too long Ted, our navigator, was brought in, but I pretended not to know him and asked 'Hello, mate, are you in the RAF?' whereupon the officer gave me a smack under the ear and said 'No more lies, he in your aeroplane!' I said that I'd never seen him before and got another smack. Later on one of the soldiers offered me a slice of black bread which I refused. The officer intervened and I told him that I'd had a good meal of bacon and eggs before I left. That earned me another almighty punch. 'Liar! England starving, England propaganda!' he screamed.

At first light they put us in a motorcycle sidecar, Ted in front and me behind, with a guard riding pillion pointing his gun at us. The guard was more concerned with hanging on than in watching us, so we were able to flip our escape gear into the hedges as we went along (we had compasses inside our buttons, the top of which unscrewed, and inside the lining of Ted's flying boots was a silk oiled map and some German currency).

We arrived at a town which I took to be Emden and came to a massive building which we soon found out was a prison. They separated me from Ted and put me in a cell. After a while they pushed an American officer in with me; he'd just been shot down. All day we had nothing to eat or drink until the evening when they brought in a bowl of watery soup and two spoons. We both started spooning up the soup as fast as we could but halfway through they dragged me out and marched me up to some offices where I was questioned by two officers. They wanted to know what plane I was flying, which squadron, my destination, who was my CO etc. After what seemed like hours of the same questions, to which I only replied with my name, rank and number, they went into a back room and left me with the girl secretary and two guards outside the door. As soon as they left, the girl jumped up, took a piece of coal from the scuttle and gave it to me for luck and said in English, 'tell them nothing.' I think she might have been Dutch.

I was returned to my cell and I had time to review the situation; everything had happened so fast that I hadn't really had time to be scared or worried yet. Late the next afternoon I was handcuffed and led out to a truck with a huge open trailer behind it. Sitting in the truck was Jock, our flight engineer, and two guards. We soon worked out that the guards didn't speak or understand English, and Jock told me that he had spent the day dragging corpses out of crashed aircraft, British and American, and they were all beneath the straw in the trailer. As we drove along every time we hit a bump you could see the corpses bounce up through the straw. In the lorry there was a flying boot with the name of our gunner, Bob Bentley, inside. The boot was full of blood and we wondered if he had been picked up and treated.

It got dark and after a couple of hours we drove along a dark tree-covered drive and pulled up outside a country house. I thought they were going to shoot us and throw us back in the trailer with the rest of them, but after a time we drove on and I breathed again. We travelled all night and arrived at a Luftwaffe base where I was put in a cell. The top window of the cell was slightly open so I could hear fighters taking off and landing. In the morning there was a gentle tap at the window, and I stretched up to see two German airmen, who gave me a lit cigarette and a meat sandwich saying 'Here, you flyer, we flyers.' Later that day I was taken to a village railway station and pushed into a little waiting room where there were about six other prisoners. After a couple of hours we heard a commotion outside; a guard who spoke English told us that an American plane had jettisoned its bombs and one had hit the local school and killed a lot of children. Not surprisingly, the locals were out to lynch us. When the train arrived, the guards formed a corridor each side and we ran across the short platform under a hail of stones and bricks, with angry people waving sticks and billhooks at us shouting 'English pigs' and 'Luft gangsters'.

The train took us to Cologne where we spent the night in a corner of the station buffet, and given more watery soup and black bread. It was an uncomfortable night, worrying that the RAF might undertake a bombing raid on Cologne. The next day we were marched to another train, with carriage benches of wooden slats, rather than the upholstered seats we were used to at home. After a longish journey we arrived at Frankfurt-am-Main. While the rest of the chaps were herded off, I was handcuffed to a soldier on each side and as we got out onto the station platform a Gestapo officer appeared, stuck a revolver in my back and we marched off towards the town. This was obviously intended to be a propaganda exercise, showing the locals that an enemy had been caught. People were shouting at me and waving their fists, and one old woman spat in my face, so I lashed out with my foot. I got my wrists nearly wrenched off and the revolver rammed painfully into my back. When we reached the town centre we boarded a queer-looking vehicle, a cross between a tram and a bus. The trolleybus took us to a grim camp, the famous Dulag Luft interrogation unit at Oberursel, where all captured Allied airmen were questioned.

We had been told in our training that if we were shot down and captured we would end up here; if they kept us for more than four days the interrogators thought we would eventually talk. I was locked up in a small cell with an intricate chromium pipe running down a corner almost to the floor. After a while this pipe started getting hotter and hotter until I began to strip off clothing. The heat then stopped and instead ice-cold air was pumped in. This regime went on day and night, while I was given the bare minimum to eat and drink. At intervals I was taken up to the interview room to be questioned by several officers, who were very courteous and pleasant, offering me cigarettes and ersatz coffee made with acorns. I answered all their questions in my broadest Kingsbridge accent, replying with 'Dunnaw, aw one o they gert big buggers' when they asked me which aircraft I had been flying, and then just my rank, name and number.

During the third day their attitude changed, and they told me that because I was only wearing a white pullover when I was caught, and not a recognised uniform, that I must be a spy. Unless I could tell them the name of my CO, and the number of my squadron and where it was based, they would have no alternative but to take me out next morning against a wall and shoot me. It seemed unlikely they would carry out this threat, as a Swiss Red Cross man had been into my cell earlier, taken my particulars and arranged for me to have a pair of shoes to replace my lost flying boots, but I spent a long night wondering what would happen in the morning. I was helped by recalling poetry I had learnt at school – *Invictus* by WE Henley: *'Out of the night that covers me, black as the pit from pole to pole, I thank whatever gods may be, for my unconquerable soul… I am the master of my fate, I am the captain of my soul'.*

The next day dawned and a chap came into my cell, an Englishman who said he was in the merchant navy. He asked a few questions which I avoided answering and then told me 'the Germans aren't such a bad lot, you know'. I suddenly realised what he was. 'You're a bloody traitor!' I shouted, and lunged towards him just as the door opened and the guards dragged him out. On another day there was a commotion outside, where an American gunner who had used the toilet was refusing to come out. Every time the guards tried to get him he shoved his hand down the toilet and threatened to throw it at them.

On the morning of the fourth day I was moved to the transit camp, in a park beside the Farben Industries head office in the centre of Frankfurt (later the headquarters of the American Forces in Europe.) I was allocated a POW number: 584. We were billeted in wooden huts, surrounded by a barbed wire fence, and at weekends the locals lined up outside the wire, to stare at us and call us 'Terror Fliegers' and 'Luft Gangsters'. Of course we couldn't resist playing up to them by running up and down the fence like monkeys.

While we were in the transit camp there was an air raid warning. Before long we heard planes in the distance, and suddenly a green target indicator dropped down across the wire, which meant it was the target for the next wave of bombers. Once again I thought this was it, blown up by our own bombers! The Americans were going crazy with fright as they had never experienced an air raid before, and we shouted at them to come into the corridor away from the glass. There were anti-aircraft guns firing just outside and the noise was deafening; then to our great relief a red TI came down to cancel the green – it seems they should have been bombing the old part of town. Another lucky escape!

After a week or so the camp was filling up with 20 to 30 airmen arriving daily from interrogation. Eventually we were marched out of camp with an armed guard of 60 soldiers, through the town to the railway sidings beyond the main platforms. I could see they were loading us into cattle trucks; I counted out 88 men per wagon. I didn't fancy being the last one in, so as the end of the queue loomed closer I bent down as if there was something wrong with my shoe, then quickly moved forward again when the last few had been shut in the truck. I was now first in the next truck. It was divided into three sections by barbed wire, with the middle section for the guards together with all our boots, braces and belts which had been taken from us as we boarded. We were shoved into the two side sections, 44 to a side.

We travelled like this for three days and nights. Once a day they threw in sour black bread and some water in a jug, and every 24 hours we stopped and were ordered '*Aus! Aus!*' We found ourselves in open countryside surrounded by guards, where we had to do our business and then get back on board. It was impossible to sleep as there was no room to lie down; we tried all ways of fitting together on the floor but the bottom ones were squashed and those on top were head-down. Two of the chaps were Canadians who had been shot down over the sea off North Africa and one of them had his arms badly burned after swimming in blazing petrol. The Germans had wrapped his burns in paper, and he couldn't put his arms against anything. One or two of us would try to hold his hands and arms clear to let him snatch some brief sleep.

I had managed to grab a place under the ventilation panel as I had been first on board, but I had to fight to keep it. I could just see out through the slats in the panel, and we often passed trains pulling endless flatbed trucks going back to Germany, each carting families of gypsies with their wagons, horses and children (we found out later that they were all going to the gas chambers). The next time we had a toilet stop we weren't shy and didn't need any urging, although we were in a triangle of grass in the centre of a small village and all the population came out to stare. We didn't care, we just dropped our trousers and got on with it, then had to queue up to be handed one or two sheets of toilet paper.

Looking out over the countryside, I was surprised that East Prussia seemed so bare, flat, and uninteresting – mile after mile of emptiness, no buildings and no people. The ground was cultivated but nobody was working. We stopped at small stations and some of our chaps who could speak a bit of German taught us to shout 'The Germans will lose the War' or 'Hitler is a pig dog.' At one station there were some prisoners being guarded by soldiers and Gestapo. The guards went mad at our taunting, and started running up and down the platform brandishing their pistols at our trucks.

At long last we reached Heydekrug and we were ordered out, collecting our shoes, belts and braces if we could find them. We fell in and were marched the six miles to the *Lager* (camp) by guards with Alsatian dogs.

7

LIFE IN THE LAGER
1943 – 1945

Stalag Luft VI, at Heydekrug, was close to the Lithuanian border, and like most prison camps was built in a clearing in a pine wood, with sandy soil that was no good for cultivation – nor very good for tunnelling. It was a massive camp consisting of three lagers: *A Lager* was for British and Commonwealth Air Force prisoners, and when we arrived it was already full so we were put in *K Lager* (I was in hut K3). There was also a Russian *Lager* and an American *Lager* somewhere close but out of sight, we could see 'ferrets' and 'hound men' going up and down a wired alleyway to them.

The prison camp was supposedly chosen for airmen because they were known to be keen escapers and it was a very long walk to Switzerland or Spain. There was another way home if you could get to Danzig (Gdansk) and watch for signals on Swedish ships: two shirts on a line meant 'come aboard', but just socks meant 'Germans on board'.

The whole of the camp was surrounded by two 15ft-high wire fences, with rolls of tangled barbed wire between. On our side of the fence, running all around the inside and about six feet from the main fence, was a 'death wire' and if you even touched that you would be shot. Every 30 to 40 yards stood a high postern box with rifles, machine guns and searchlights, and these were manned day and night. The huts were built in blocks of ten, each hut containing 72 men. They were raised up above the ground and had a door beneath at each end; these doors allowed the hound men to send the dogs in at one end and meet them at the other, to check if any of us were tunnelling underneath the hut. Sometimes a boiler-suited ferret would crawl beneath the hut, which is how they got their nickname.

The huts were long and narrow, with doors at both ends and a window at the front. They were built of rough stone, lime-washed inside, with wooden floors and a flat-topped stone stove. In a tiny room at the back was a bucket for toilet use at night. There were one or two rough tables with benches, and 18 wooden double-bunkbeds down each side. Each bed had one thin blanket which you could see through, and we slept on straw palliasses. We were covered in fleas and lice, although they didn't bother me too much. Our diet consisted of watery soups of varying descriptions, black bread and margarine like cart grease, and every now and then 'jam' made from beetroot and sugar beet. We were never issued with any crockery or cutlery; we made our own out of Red Cross tins.

Twice a day we were taken out of the huts for *Appell* – rollcall – and after the evening count we were shut in until the next morning. When night fell, the floodlights would be switched on and guard dogs were let loose in the compound – and occasionally into the huts, where you would be attacked if you were out of your bed. Two dogs were once let loose in the Russian lager, and they disappeared. Days later the bones were thrown out over the fence, sucked clean of marrow.

Once a week a man was chosen from each hut to go out on wood patrol – six men for six huts. We would be harnessed to a flatbed cart, with three men on each side, and would haul the cart out into the forest where we would break off dead branches from the trees with our bare hands, whilst being guarded by some old boys who sat around smoking as they watched us. On our return we shared the firewood between the six huts, but there was only enough to last one evening – the rest of the week we froze. On one firewood trip, two of us arranged for the other four to cover for us, and we managed to sneak off into the wood, coming to a clearing with a farmhouse in the distance and a large mound. We crawled on our bellies towards the mound, keeping it between us and the house, and dug into it, hoping to find potatoes, but instead discovered sugarbeet. We grabbed as many as we could carry and got back without being missed. We smuggled the beet back to the camp under the firewood, and fried it in margarine on our homemade blower. This was made out of Red Cross tins, and wood and nails pinched from the bed slats. It consisted of a baseboard on which was a housing which contained a handle and a circular fan. When turned by the handle, the fan blew a draught along a tube and up under a firebox the size of a steamed pudding can – it was surprising what you could cook with just one or two chips of wood. Most huts had versions of these, and some engineering nits invented gears for theirs, but when the handle was turned it blew the fuel right out of the firebox.

We sorted ourselves into 'combines' of two to six or seven men. There were six in our combine; one did the cleaning, one went out to scrounge wood for the blower, I did the cooking, and so on.

Now and then, early in the morning, the hut door would open and the guards would burst in bellowing '*Raus! Raus!*' and we would jump out and stand by our bunks while they searched our bodies, clothing and beds, then we were turned outside in all weathers, sometimes for the whole day, while they searched the huts. They knew we had a radio but they could never find it – it was hidden inside an accordion which could still be played. Each night some of the chaps went to a secret lair under one of the huts and plugged into the German mains supply to get the midnight World News from the BBC. This was then dictated to a few news

52. Like many POWs, Bill kept a Wartime Log, using a notebook supplied to British prisoners by the YMCA, together with coloured pencils and ink, distributed through the Red Cross system. With watercolours extracted from food can labels and paintbrushes made from their own hair, prisoners used these books for sketches, cartoons, maps, poems and diary entries.

Bill's log has illustrations drawn by himself and his fellow POWs, as well as popular poems and prose which were shared amongst the POW fraternity.

Blue Skies of Exile

Only to the earth am I imprisoned,
   There is no fixity about the sky,
For often upwards from the barbed fence gazing,
   I see a bit of native air roll by,
Breathed into, brightened by two hearts I left behind me,
   And I think sometimes the sky has caught
The very prayers that you are speaking
   In answer to the light-winged homing thoughts
Which I release to Heaven now and then
   In supplication that an errant star
May drop them off when in its orbit flying,
   He passes o'er the garden where you are.
Only to the earth am I imprisoned
   And sometimes when the sky is special blue
I know it is the self-same piece of Heaven
   That yesterday sailed slowly over you.

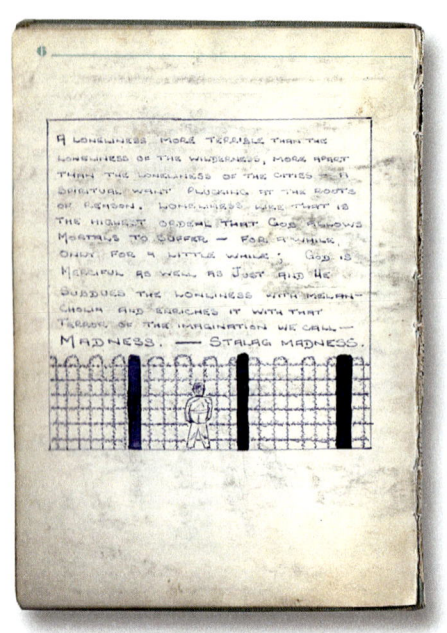

53 & 54. The righthand page reads: 'A loneliness more terrible than the loneliness of the wilderness, more apart than the loneliness of the cities – a spiritual want plucking at the roots of reason. Loneliness like that is the highest ordeal that God allows mortals to suffer – for a while, only for a litte while; God is merciful as well as just and He subdues the loneliness with melancholia and enriches it with that terror of the imagination we call – MADNESS – STALAG MADNESS.'

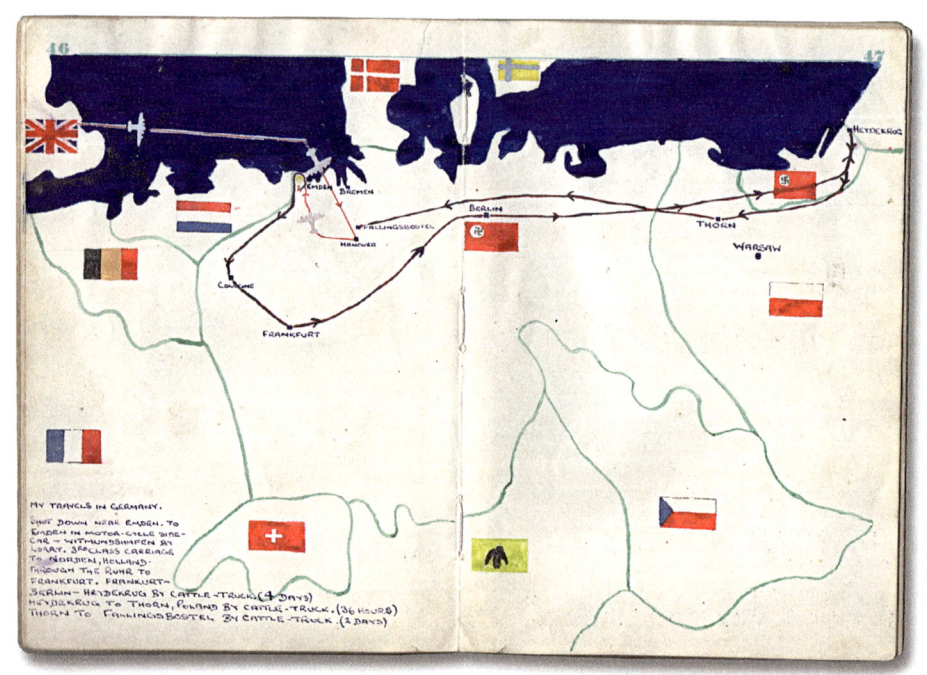

55. Bill's hand-drawn map showing 'my travels in Germany', part of his Wartime Log.

Sgt. W. E. Warren, R.A.F.

Missing Man is Prisoner of War

Information has been received that Sergt. "Bill" Warren, of the R.A.F., who was reported missing late in September, is now a prisoner of war in Germany. His mother, Mrs. E. C. Warren, of Wallingford Road, Kingsbridge, has received a postcard from him, saying that he is safe and uninjured. Mrs. Warren has received many letters expressing sympathy, and as it is impossible for her to answer all of them, she would like, through the "Gazette," to thank all who have written.

Missing Airman.

Sergt. W. E. Warren, who, as reported last week, is now a prisoner of war in Germany, is the husband of Mrs. Warren, of 2, Magdala Cottage, Devon Road, Salcombe, who wishes to thank all kind friends for their letters of sympathy. Mr. and Mrs. Warren were married in 1940, and Sergt. Warren visited his home in Salcombe only about a week before he was reported missing in September.

DEATH OF MR. E. C. WARREN

Many in the town will learn with regret of the death, on Wednesday, of Mr. Ernest Charles Warren, of 33, Wallingford-road, Kingsbridge.

Known to his friends as "Ern," Mr. Warren was much respected. He had been seriously ill for several months, and passed away at Hawkmoor Sanatorium. For 30 years he was employed as clerk by Messrs. Oke Bros., Ltd., of Bridge-street.

During the last war Mr. Warren was a sergeant-instructor in the Royal Corps of Signals, seeing service in India and Palestine. In this war, until illness laid him aside, he again did his bit. He held the rank of sergeant in the Signals Section of the Home Guard.

The widow's loss is shared by a daughter and two sons, the eldest of whom is a prisoner of war in Germany.

The funeral takes place to-morrow (Saturday) at Dodbrooke Parish Church, at 2.30 p.m.

Left: news of Bill's fate reaches home. Above: while Bill was a prisoner of war, his father, Ern, passed away.

56 & 57. In July 1944, with the Russians fast advancing, Stalag Luft VI at Heydekrug was evacuated. Bill and his mates were marched and then transported by cattle truck to Stalag 357 at Thorn, in Poland. Within just a few weeks they were moved by cattle truck west to Fallingbostel, where Stalag 357 was relocated on the site of Stalag XI-D.

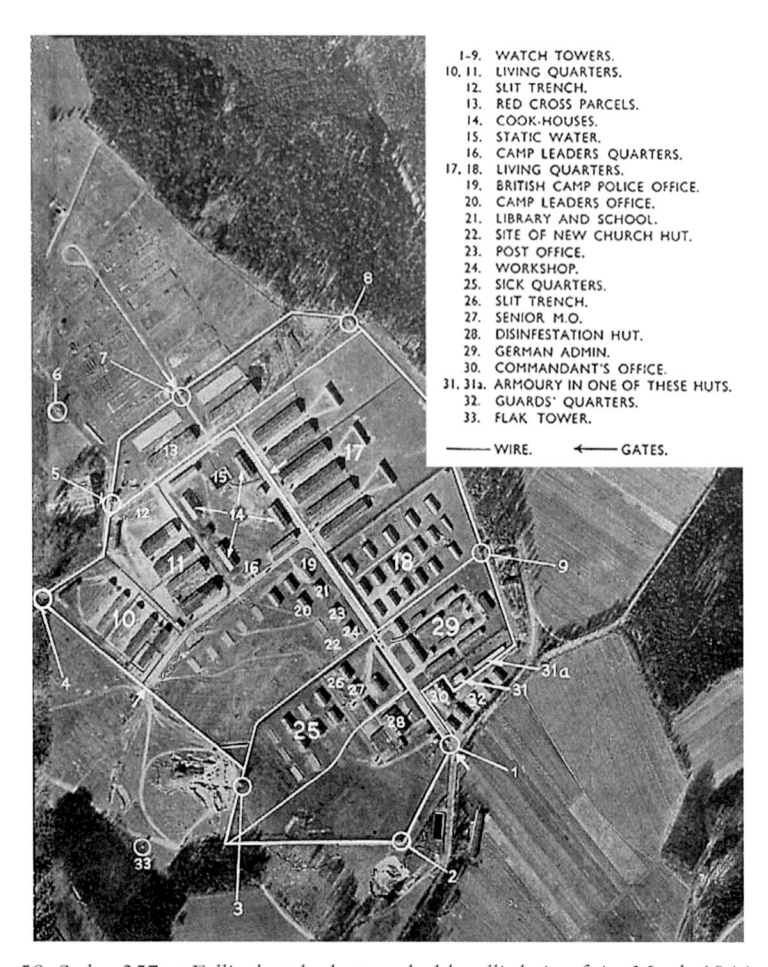

```
1-9.     WATCH TOWERS.
10, 11.  LIVING QUARTERS.
12.      SLIT TRENCH.
13.      RED CROSS PARCELS.
14.      COOK-HOUSES.
15.      STATIC WATER.
16.      CAMP LEADERS QUARTERS.
17, 18.  LIVING QUARTERS.
19.      BRITISH CAMP POLICE OFFICE.
20.      CAMP LEADERS OFFICE.
21.      LIBRARY AND SCHOOL.
22.      SITE OF NEW CHURCH HUT.
23.      POST OFFICE.
24.      WORKSHOP.
25.      SICK QUARTERS.
26.      SLIT TRENCH.
27.      SENIOR M.O.
28.      DISINFESTATION HUT.
29.      GERMAN ADMIN.
30.      COMMANDANT'S OFFICE.
31, 31a. ARMOURY IN ONE OF THESE HUTS.
32.      GUARDS' QUARTERS.
33.      FLAK TOWER.

———— WIRE.    ←———— GATES.
```

58. *Stalag 357 at Fallingbostel, photographed by allied aircraft in. March 1944.*

59. *On 16 April 1945, a recce group of 8th Hussars reached the two Fallingbostel camps – XI-B and XI-D/357 (Bill's camp). The camps were the first British POW camps to be liberated.*

60, 61 & 62. Liberated POWs at Fallingbostel: at Stalag XI-B (above left) and at Stalag 357 (above right and below), including those in the sick bay.

63. Bill's discharge papers, dated 11 July 1945, giving the date of his liberation from Fallingbostel as 28 April 1945.

64. Back from the war. Bill (third from left) with his sister Una, mother Flo, and brother Alan. Bill's daughter Sandra sits in the front, in front of Bill.

65. Bill at Lannacombe Bay, 1964

66. Bill in Canada, 1985

67. Bill as teacher at Penryn

68. Marion, Richard, Alison, Bill and Michael, 1980

69. Marion and Bill

70. Bill and Linda, 1985

71. Bill with his sister Una and his brother Alan, in the 1980s.

72. Bill in The Mikado, performed by Helston School Gilbert & Sullivan Society, 1984.

73. Bill with Cornishman Sandy Rowe. Sandy was a fellow prisoner at Stalag Luft VI. He had been shot down just a few days before Bill, on 23 September 1943, on a raid over Mannheim, in his Lancaster bomber.

74. Bill in the late 90s, outside his home in Carnkie, Cornwall, wearing his medals on Remembrance Day.

readers who went round the huts reading it to us while look-outs were posted outside. If any guards approached, the look-outs would cry 'Goons up!' Some of the goons were OK though, and could be bribed with cigarettes to bring in parts for the radio, maps or even civilian clothes.

The latrines were 50 yards away from the huts – a miserable walk in the winter months of snow, mud and slush. Even so, they turned out to be the best we were to experience compared with later camps. They consisted of a long wooden box with 16 holes cut either side so that 32 men could sit down at once. Every other day a guard would arrive with a tank pulled by two Friesian oxen. He would fill a small container on the side of the tank then light it, and this would get the suction going to pump up the slurry from the pit and into the tank. When it was full it was taken outside the gate and around to the windward side of the compound and spread on the ground. In the summer the smell was rank! One hot day there was an outbreak of dysentery, and I ran down to the toilet to find every hole taken and a queue of men waiting with their belts undone. I was standing in the queue and saw a Canadian friend put his cigarette end down between his legs, and the next second there was an almighty explosion and every single man jumped up grabbing their rear. Because every hole was being covered in quick succession the methane gas had built up inside and the glowing cigarette end had set the gas alight. I laughed so much I nearly had an accident.

The terms of the Geneva Convention were that POWs should receive the same rations as the base troops, but the Germans didn't stick to the rules. Our daily ration was a tin cup of watery potato soup and a two-inch thick slice of sour black bread. Sometimes the bread tasted like pine trees because they had eked out the flour with pine sawdust. Once a week we got a lump of fatty, stinking horsemeat, or a piece of *Wurst* – sausage – made from animal lungs. Once they told us we were getting mushrooms the next day, but some of the chaps went to investigate and found a barrel of stinking runny mushrooms. Another time we were promised pork, and Jock (our flight engineer who had been a meat inspector in Edinburgh) went to the cookhouse to spy on the meat arriving. He saw six pig carcasses so thin that they must have died from TB. We were often given food that was too bad for the guards to eat; we were even issued with razorblades which the German soldiers had already used.

When we had Red Cross parcels delivered we then had enough energy to walk round and round the compound wire. There'd be hundreds of us, in groups of two or three, all walking anti-clockwise. We even managed a bit of rugby with a stone wrapped in sacking. We should have had a parcel each, delivered weekly, but usually it would be one parcel each a month, or one between four (and once, a parcel which I had to divide between 16 of us). The best parcels came from Canada, with a pound tin of solid jam and a large tin of Borden's Klim which was by far the best milk powder. If you wanted to swap a tin of Klim for one of Nestlé from the American parcels you would expect to pay an extra 20 cigarettes as well. The English parcels were understandably poor, due to rationing at home, and only contained a couple of ounces of marg and sugar, or a small tin three-quarters full of thin runny jam. The American parcels were good but they wasted a lot of space with chewing gum, and who wants that when you're starving?

Now and then a bulk delivery of cigarettes would arrive. Perhaps two hundred thousand would be sent from England, but by the time our dockers had taken a cut, then the Portuguese dockers and railmen, and then the Germans, when they reached us less than a quarter of the original consignment would be left. One day we had food from the English-speaking people of Argentina; I remember eating a slice of cheese which was delicious, but where it touched my lips and cheeks I soon came out in a rash, probably due to the salt which we were unused to.

We had an elected camp leader, or 'man of confidence' whose name was 'Dixie' Deans. He'd been a prisoner for four years and spoke fluent German which enabled him to negotiate with the Germans on our behalf [Sergeant James Deans of 77 Squadron had been captured after crash-landing at Venebrugge in September 1940 and became a renowned camp leader, first at Stalag Luft III and later at Stalag Luft VI; in March 1945, Deans took charge of 2,000 POWs on 'The Long March' across Poland and Germany to Stalag 357 at Fallingbostel]. The first German commandant we had wasn't bad, and Dixie was able to arrange for a big empty hut to become our theatre-cum-recreation hall. But after a while he was moved away for being pro-British and was replaced by an ogre with a face right out of a horror story. His face was like a skeleton with sunken cheeks and staring eyes.

We always gave the Germans a rough time and even when we weren't preparing to escape we fooled them into thinking that we were, which kept as many guards as possible occupied, leaving fewer to kill our compatriots on other fronts. We had an escape committee and every idea had to go before them to be sanctioned, preventing any crazy ideas messing up one already in progress. We always had several tunnels on the go, supervised by former trainee surveyors and mining engineers. Tunnelling was a rotten job as we were naked, working in the dim light provided by clarified margarine in a two-ounce butter tin with a wick made from a piece of braces. Air was pumped along the tunnel through joined-together jam tins, by a chap at the other end squeezing an old accordion. Before you could become a tunneller you had to pass a thorough medical examination by the British MO. There was a tunnel five huts up from us, where they had taken some blocks out of the side of the stove and fixed them to a board which acted as a door. They were well out under the first wire when the goons raided the hut and went straight to the door. It turned out that we'd had a German spy with us whom we thought was a Pole. Some of the men set upon him but the guards dragged him out quickly. Then the Germans dug down to the tunnel and emptied the contents of the latrine tanker into it. The poor chaps had to live with the smell for months.

When we were out for *Appell* we stood in our hut groups around the square, with the German officers in the middle, whilst we were being counted by *Feldwebels* – sergeants. It was easy for us to move about in the ranks and mess up the count so that they never knew just how many there were. This made them mad, and so they decided to try a 'sheep count' whereby we were supposed to funnel between two hurdles one at a time. When they had fixed up the hurdles the signal was given and we all made a run for the other side of the square, making sheep noises as we went. They called in armed reinforcements who ran into the *Lager* and moved the hurdles to the other end again, but we galloped back with the soldiers hitting anyone they could with their rifle butts. We finally gave up but we'd enjoyed the fun!

We often gave the guards a hard time during *Appell*. If it was deep snow they were pelted with snowballs but they couldn't tell where the missiles came from; at other times it would be small stones which stung their bodies. The Gestapo wore jackboots, short fur coats and trilby hats with a feather stuck in the hat band. Once, when they were searching our hut, an officer took off his coat and left it on a bunk; needless to say, when he came to fetch it later it had vanished. Within a few days some of the chaps were wearing fancy caps made from the coat! We found out where most of the Guards lived and teased them by saying 'I hear that last night the RAF bombed Leipzig' – or Cologne, or Hamburg.

Getting rid of fresh sand from the tunnels posed a problem, but we disposed of some by arranging for two men to start a fight in front of a postern tower. A mass of chaps crowded around shouting encouragement, while others with sandbags beneath their greatcoats pulled a string to release the sand. The crowd scuffled and stamped it underfoot, mingling it with the sandy soil. The tunnellers once came across a massive boulder in their path, and they decided the best way to dispose of it was the most obvious; they dragged it up into the hut and when the coast was clear they left it outside the front door. The Germans didn't notice it for weeks.

I watched one man escape; he was called Grimshaw and had relations who lived at Batson, near Salcombe. He had been a prisoner since 1940 and had tried to escape many times – you could say he was 'escape crazy' – and had learned to speak almost perfect German. The escape committee told us that something was going to happen but we should ignore it and not stare. I was doing the usual circuit around the wire when I noticed Grimshaw wearing imitation goon overalls near the gate. He had mock earphones on and was carrying a box just like the guards did, which they clipped to the wire to listen for vibrations from any tunnelling below. He had timed it for the lunchtime change of guard, and he climbed up between the wires and stood on a plank (which had previously been sawn partway through). The plank broke and in perfect German he said to the guard 'Ah well, I'll come back after lunch'. The guard opened the gate and the last we saw of him he was walking across the empty *Lager* beyond the fence.

After the war, when I was back in Salcombe, his mother came to visit me. She'd received a letter from a chap in the south of

France, who Grimshaw had hidden with for a few days on his flight to Spain. He'd left to catch a train, and later that same day the train came steaming past the village, with Grimshaw clinging to the outside, as German soldiers leaned out of the carriage windows firing at him. She still hoped that somehow he'd survived, and perhaps had escaped and was now a prisoner of the Russians.

Some POWs developed what we called 'wire disease' or 'Kriegie madness' (from the German *Kriegsgefangener* – prisoner of war). One morning an Australian chap couldn't stand it anymore, and jumped out of the window and ran for the wire. The men in his hut shouted '*Kopf Krank!*' (head sickness) but the Guards opened fire when he was halfway up the wire and shot him dead.

Life in the *Lager* was one long bore. We spent a lot of time sleeping so that we could forget how cold and hungry we were. I was so bored that I invented a crazy way to occupy my time. Lying on the top bunk I watched the very large blowflies above me, and managing to catch one, I pulled a fine thread out of an old shirt and tied it to one of the fly's legs. The other end was fixed to a splinter on the beam above and I watched the insect fly around until it was exhausted. Then I released it and caught another.

When we first entered *K Lager* there was grass growing in the compound. We tried cooking it on our blower but it didn't go far and wasn't very filling. In the spring we caught some frogs in a swamp at the bottom of the compound, and a Polish prisoner prepared them for us. Cooked on the blower, they tasted delicious. We even tried our hand at catching some of the many starlings. Behind the latrines, we fixed a bowl propped up on a stick with a long thread attached, and as bait we sacrificed a bit of our precious bread. Watching from around a corner, we pulled the thread to trap the starling. We caught and cooked several until the guards put a stop to it, claiming the starling was a protected bird in Germany.

Hearing a commotion outside one night we all ran to the window, to see a 'ferret' being attacked by a guard dog in the corridor between the wires leading to the American *Lager* – there must have been a mistake in the timing of the patrol handover. The houndman had a struggle to get the dog off the ferret.

The dogs were trained by holding them outside the wire and pointing at us while beating the hell out of them with a stick. One night I opened the window to throw out some water and a pair of jaws snapped shut, missing my arm by inches! The Swiss Red Cross sent us some packets of vegetable seeds so we made little gardens up against the internal wire. Later we were given some tins of fish which the German troops wouldn't eat. We were starving but it was so strong and salty that we couldn't stomach it either, but rather than waste it we dug it into our veg patches to form humus. It seemed a good idea but that night the dogs dug it up and ate it with our seeds as well.

One occasion which stands out in my memory was Christmas Eve, 1943. We were in our bunks when the public address speakers started blaring out 'Silent Night'. Rushing to the windows we watched a German dressed as Old Father Time, complete with scythe, running around the compound in the searchlight beams. I think this was the only time we all applauded our enemies.

On Christmas Day and Hitler's birthday (20 April) we were given pig's blood and barley – pearl barley that had been cooked in large boilers, with a couple of buckets of pig's blood stirred into it. Disgusting as it was, when there had been no Red Cross parcels for weeks we would eat almost anything to relieve the hunger. It tasted a bit like pork but the blood stuck to our mouths and lips, and we would be sucking it off for ages. Every now and then the potato soup was changed to swede and when they threw the skins out of the cookhouse window there'd be scores of us outside with our Red Cross tins ready to collect the peelings to cook up on our blowers. It just showed how thin our veneer of civilisation was, as we fought and growled at each other to grab as many turnip skins as we could. Afterwards, the camp discipline committee issued an order that only one man per hut would be allowed to grab the skins. Guess who my hut chose?

When I first arrived at Heydekrug we were allowed to visit prisoners in *A Lager*, a few of us at a time. There, to my total surprise, I came across Jeff Watson, whose parents kept the *King's Arms* in Salcombe. He had been shot down in April 1940 and had been a prisoner for more than three years; he was a bit 'wirey' but recognised me. Much later, I was playing 'rugby' and I had just scored a try when a voice from the other side of the wire said 'What are you doing down there, Bill Warren?' Looking up I saw a familiar-looking chap on the fenced-off path between the two *Lagers*, pulling a handcart loaded with Red Cross parcels. It was Stan Pryor, who'd married May Steer from Kingsbridge, and he threw me a toothbrush and a razor (after the war he set up a car-spraying business in our old stables).

When there was an outbreak of typhoid in the Russian *Lager*, a notice went up to say there was sufficient vaccine for a limited number of injections. I persuaded our combine to go straight down to the MO but even so I was surprised that a few didn't bother. We were jabbed in the buttock and it felt like stinging nettles were spreading under the skin.

Evacuation to Thorn and Fallingbostel

One summer night, in July 1944, we heard the rumble of heavy guns in the distance and realised it must be the advancing Russian artillery. The rumbling went on all day and at nightfall we were told to make arrangements to evacuate. The word went around to destroy everything we couldn't carry. I remember standing outside our hut skimming our few gramophone records like Frisbees. And then we marched out of the camp.

Some of the men who were long-term prisoners had accumulated a fair amount of stuff through swapping and bartering cigarettes to buy things from the Germans. After a couple of days marching they began to dump things bit by bit. There were guards to either side of us and houndmen at the rear, making the dogs bite at the stragglers to keep them going. Our combine tried to keep up at the front, as it was all too easy to slip further and further behind, but even so I had to keep going back to force Jock Harvey to keep up with us. At night we were pushed into a field, or a compound on the way, given a boiled potato in its skin and a dipper full of water.

I forget how many days we marched south like this but eventually we were corralled into a railway siding to await the inevitable train of cattle trucks. We were bundled into the trucks and travelled on for 36 hours; stopping, starting, getting out to relieve ourselves, getting pushed into overgrown sidings, until finally we disembarked and were marched through the streets of a town to reach an ex-army compound. On our way through the town a woman rushed off the pavement and threw her arms around one of the Polish chaps; it was her son. The guards jumped on her and pulled her roughly away.

We had fetched up in a place called Thorn (now Torun), in Poland, about 180 miles northwest of Warsaw, in Stalag 357. Here the compound defences seemed laughable to us as there was only one wire fence. As soon as I got inside I went off on a recce to find the best hut, and while I was doing this some lowlife pinched my trousers which I'd left with the others (as it was summer we were all wearing tattered cut-off shorts). This wasn't a good start, and I was later to spend the first few months of winter on *Appell* twice a day still in shorts with my legs freezing. It wasn't until February that a replacement pair of trousers finally arrived, when the Red Cross parcels caught up with our movements from camp to camp. We were also issued with airforce Glengarry caps.

One evening we were busy making forbidden margarine candles, when I sneaked outside in the dark before curfew. I turned my Glengarry backwards so that it looked like a German hat, poked my head half up into the window and shouted *'Leichten Aus!'* – lights out. There was a mad scuffle inside to douse the candles. I waited a little while then walked into the hut and lit a candle. Instant panic and shouts of 'You'll get us shot!' A couple of chaps even dropped to the floor in anticipation. I couldn't pretend innocence for long as I was bursting with laughter. I had to suffer several practical jokes to make up for it later.

The camp was next to a road with a railway line some distance to the other side. In the mornings, lorry-loads of Polish girls would pass by on their way to work, and in the evenings they returned and would throw apples over the fence to us. On Sunday afternoons they would often pick wild flowers on the bank outside the wire fence, bending over with their skirts pulled up to show us their knickers. It was all wasted on us; when you're starving you crave only food, and our main hobby was collecting recipes from the chaps who knew these things. Every day we saw younger boys and girls herding huge flocks of geese out on to the flat grassland area. Poland was a depressing dark, grey-green country which seemed to be always in low cloud and drizzle.

While we were in Thorn we often saw bright lights shooting across the sky, faster than any aircraft could travel. They were travelling towards the Russian zone, and we found out later that they were the prototype V-2 rockets. By now, most of us were not bothered about escaping, as all the Russian activity indicated that the war would soon be over. Some men did manage to escape and were hidden by locals in the underground tunnels and passages for which the town was famous. When the Germans threatened to shoot ten townspeople on every day that the prisoners were out, the men returned to the camp.

We had only been at Thorn a few weeks when we once again heard the distant noise of the Russian forces advancing, and it was time to move out. We were marched back to the rail sidings and into the cattle trucks for another long, uncomfortable, hungry journey right across Poland, and halfway across northern Germany. Two days later we arrived at Fallingbostel [there was a large complex of barracks and camps here, including Stalag XI-B and XI-D; after the evacuation from Thorn, the latter camp was generally known as Stalag 357, which was Bill Warren's camp].

Fallingbostel was in the centre of a triangle between Hanover, Magdeburg and Celle. Our *Lager* was made up of the usual wooden barrack blocks and a large shed with cold water taps over wooden troughs which were freezing in winter. The latrine was a massive hole in the ground with a galvanised iron roof and no sides. We sat on rustic poles over the hole, in winter brown stalagmites crept upwards. It was so cold that several of us would 'save it up' and go together to keep each other warm.

One day the Germans told us to bring our palliasses outside and they would give us new ones. We piled the mattresses up in a heap and they set them alight while we returned to our compound and waited for replacements to arrive. Then they announced over the loudspeakers that we wouldn't be getting any, as retribution for German POWs who had been forced to sleep in tents on the sand in North Africa. That left us with nothing to sleep on but bare boards, some of which were missing because they'd been used in tunnelling activities. We had no fat on our bodies at all, and we were soon covered in sores.

A daylight air raid by American planes sent us all scurrying into our huts. There was a lot of noise from machine guns above and anti-aircraft guns on the ground, and everyone wanted to know what was happening, so I climbed out the window and was busy giving a running commentary when I got caught by two guards. I refused to answer their questions, only giving the stock answer 'Joe Soap' when asked for my name, and when they demanded to see my identity disc, I entered a different hut to fetch it, then ran out the back door and in again through another one. Other prisoners deliberately got in their way and the guards soon lost me. I thought I had got away with it but a few days later one of the sergeants on *Appell* recognised me and I was marched off to solitary in a cell for seven days.

There was a well-organised swap shop at Fallingbostel, an area in the washhouse where the wheeler-dealers could lay out their stuff for trading and swapping. I managed to get a racket going there too. The Germans had cartloads of swedes delivered to the cookhouse regularly and as they passed the huts I would run out and grab a couple of swedes, nip across the road and disappear between the huts while the others in the combine got in the way of any guards in pursuit. The swedes we didn't want we exchanged for other things.

There was an empty compound beside us and one winter's day they drove in hundreds of Polish people – old men and women, children and mothers with babies. They had no shelter at all and the weather was bitter and sleet was falling. They just lay in the mud when they were exhausted. Although we were starving we threw our bread ration over the wire fence to them until the guards in the towers started firing at us. These poor souls stayed there for three or four days, until they were told they were going down the road for a bath and warm huts, but of course they were going to the gas chambers.

Liberation

By the beginning of April 1945, the whole camp site had become a sea of mud. I developed asthma, which I'd had as a child, and was put into the medical hut under the care of our MO Major Bonham-Carter [Richard Bonham-Carter was MO for the 4th Parachute Brigade, 1st Airborne Division, and had been captured during the battle for Arnhem, 1944]. He was very sympathetic, as his mother also suffered from asthma, and the only medicine he had was a box of honey, lemon and ipecacuanha cough syrup which tasted like nectar to my sugar-starved body. While I was in the sick-bay the order came to evacuate the camp as the 8th Army was approaching. The sick, including me, were to be left behind.

My Salcombe mate Jeff Watson came to see me before he left, I tried to persuade him to hide with me beneath the floorboards and wait for the allied troops to release us, but he replied 'I've been a prisoner for nearly five years and I don't want to take any chances. I'll go out with the main party and play it safe'. He left, and with Ted, my old navigator, marched off with other POWs in columns of 500, along roads crowded with lorries, wagons and retreating German soldiers. They were passing through woods when several men tried to escape, only to be shot by the guards and tied to trees as a warning to others. On 19 April, they were marching towards the village of Gresse when six RAF Typhoons flew in low over them and opened fire, thinking they were Germans, and killed 36 of them. Ted later told me that he'd thrown himself into a ditch, but shrapnel caught Jeff in the temple and killed him instantly.

I recovered from my asthma in a couple of days to find there were only 30 or 40 of us left in the camp. All of a sudden we found ourselves in the middle of a battlefield, and a few of us climbed onto the hut roof for a better view. British tanks were approaching along the road and a group of German soldiers emerged from the woods waving white handkerchiefs tied to their rifles. Then a German tank roared past and they all ran back into the woods ripping the handkerchiefs away. We were laughing and cheering until a shell swished past our heads and in two seconds we were underneath the hut!

After a short while two scout cars from the 8th Hussars drove into the camp, and we all gathered round. The officer in charge had tears in his eyes as he mumbled that he never thought he'd see British troops in such a state; we were very thin and in filthy rags. Not long after a lorry arrived and dished out freshly-baked white bread. I've never tasted anything so delicious – we ate it dry, and it tasted like the best cake! The Germans had moved hundreds of Russian prisoners into the empty huts left after our men were evacuated, and as soon as the camp was liberated and the gates were open, the Russians took carts and horses and went out to raid the nearby village, returning with all kinds of furniture. They also raped local women and several of them killed a teenage girl when they had finished with her. Thankfully they were only held at Fallingbostel for a few days.

Whilst we were prisoners, it had been the habit of one old German farmer who lived nearby to walk outside the perimeter fence, especially on Sundays, and stand laughing and patting his fat stomach to taunt us. I always said I would get him when we were released. I persuaded one of the British soldiers to lend me his rifle and a few of us, including Jock Harvey, went out to the farm. Old Fatty saw us coming and fled indoors. With the help of an old iron mangle we broke our way inside, and discovered the farmer and his wife were standing up against the fireplace with their hands up, shaking with fright. I stood in front of them and patted my stomach so they knew why we were there. Jock tried asking for eggs, but his German wasn't good enough and the old woman took the clock off the mantelpiece and gave it to him. Hanging above the mantle was a double-barrel shotgun which I grabbed, telling him they wouldn't be needing that any more. When we found a goose in the yard, the woman pleaded with us to leave it, but we cornered and killed it. Back at the camp, I lit a fire to cook the bird, which the others had plucked, and about eight of us shared it, but soon afterwards we were bringing it all back up! Major Bonham-Carter told us that our stomachs would take a long time to cope with rich food like that, and could only digest very small amounts at a time.

We heard about a large German warehouse, up a steep hill near the village. There were scores of different compartments inside, storing hardware, tools and comforts for the German forces. Finally we located the food stores and loaded up with as much as we could carry in our weakened condition. We took oats, flour, margarine, sugar and dried fruit, and later I mixed up a sort of cake-like porridge while the others lit a fire. We found a tin in the cookhouse and baked our concoction. It tasted good but once again everyone was violently sick. We still hadn't learned our lesson,

A new army officer arrived, the new military governor of the area. He saw the shotgun I had pinched from the farmer and told me that he was billeted in a large house on the hill, which had a room full of top-class rifles and Zeiss binoculars, and suggested that we might be able to get some items back to England. We could go up to the house the next day and take our pick. We didn't get the chance, as a fleet of ambulances arrived next morning and we had to grab our few belongings and move out.

The convoy of ambulances stopped during the journey so we could get out and relieve ourselves, right outside a farm. Within minutes there were 20 or so hens all up in the air and we were knocking them down with sticks or anything else we could grab. As we drove on, we left a trail of feathers behind us as we plucked them. We were taken to a big base hospital at Diepholz and had chicken for lunch the next day.

Three or four of us escaped through a window and went for a walk in the town, still in our rags; the locals ran into alleyways or houses in utter panic. We were climbing back through the window when we realised that everyone else was on parade, holding a draw to sort out places in aircraft to fly us home. The weather was bad and they could only spare a few Dakotas for the trip. I drew number 15 but Ted Bamsey drew 250.

We took off the next day and the pilot made a sweeping detour to show us the mess the tanks had made all around the Rhine. We landed at RAF Lyneham, where we had our first bath in over two years, with a WAAF in attendance because we were very weak and likely to fall over. The hot water turned me into a red lobster which was quite alarming. I rang the bell and my attendant came in to reassure me that it was the usual reaction since we had not experienced hot water, let alone a bath, for so long.

After a few days' rest we were transferred by ambulance to the RAF Hospital at Hednesford. I had gained a little weight by now, but I still weighed only eight-and-a-half stone, and was so weak that I could only walk 40 or 50 yards without collapsing. Whilst we were there we could ring the bell beside our bed, day or night, and they would cook us anything we fancied. We were strolling about the base when a newly-joined flying officer thought he was going to march us about. When we fell in, he shouted 'left turn', and we fell about laughing; one of the chaps replied 'Bullshit' and another said 'Look here, mate, we've been chased around by the Germans for years, we're not putting up with it here!' And from then on we walked everywhere instead of marching in three lines.

After a week the doctors carried out fitness tests to make sure we were fit enough to travel home, as many POWs had been collapsing on trains and in stations. One test was to step up onto a chair and down again ten times. I was sure I could do it, but I ended up on the floor after only three steps. Eventually I was deemed fit enough but only on the condition that I would travel to London and spend the night there, before travelling on to Kingsbridge the next day.

Before leaving Hednesford we were de-mobbed and collected our 'civvies'. I remember I chose a chalk-striped grey suit and a trilby hat. On 11 July 1945 I was discharged.

Coming home

When the train pulled in at Kingsbridge station I was overwhelmed by the crowds of family, friends and townspeople who were there to welcome me.

For the first three months at home returning POWs were allowed double rations, and our families received letters explaining to them to 'handle us with care'. Salcombe was still full of American GIs then, and I was introduced to some of them one night. The next day there was a knock at the door, and one of the Yanks was on the doorstep with a tray of turkey breasts. Their medical officer had advised them that white meat in moderation was best for an ex-POW. This was followed over the next few weeks by pork chops, tins of Spam, tins of pineapple and fruit salad, sealed tins of matches and even a pair of thigh boots.

The Americans knew I was keen on shooting so one day they

turned up with a Springfield rifle and 1000 rounds of ammunition. We took the rifle out to Bearscombe Farm and set up a drum of water on one side of the valley, then went over to the other side about a quarter of a mile away. We eventually hit the drum but the next day a mate asked 'Was that you firing a rifle at Bearscombe?' He'd heard it in Kingsbridge!

As soon as I got stronger I started work, crabbing with George Clements. Being at sea every morning and hauling crab pots soon got me back to normal. One day I reluctantly took the rifle out to sea and chucked it overboard with the remaining rounds – the police were on the lookout for illegal firearms. The seabed off Salcombe was littered with everything you could think of. When the Americans left they off-loaded their excess equipment into the bay; they'd been told that taking supplies home involved a lot of red tape so they ditched it all quickly. Fishermen in the area trawled up a lot of usable goods although there was always a risk of booby traps.

The *King's Arms* in Salcombe was still run by the parents of Jeff Watson, my fellow POW who'd been killed by friendly fire on the road to Gresse. Soon after I returned home I visited them and they took me upstairs to show me what they had kept for him on his return – the chocolate and crystallised fruit they had managed to save from their meagre rations. His clothes were pressed and laid out on his bed, and his polished shoes were lined up together on the bedroom floor.

EPILOGUE
by MARION WARREN

LIFE IN PEACETIME 1945 – 2007

Following his return to Devon, Bill faced a long period of recovery both physical and mental. After two years of starvation he was unable to eat a normal diet without nausea or bloating. It took time for him to regain a healthy weight and rebuild his muscular physique and strength. Bill also had to adjust to family life. Whilst on leave in 1940 he had married Judy, and in his absence his daughter Sandra had arrived and his father had died from TB. No doubt his relationship with his wife Judy had suffered, as so many others had, as a result of the wartime separation.

After the war there was a desperate need for teachers, and the government set up a fast-track course to train anyone suitable. Bill applied and was sent to Wadsworth College in London to complete a course which qualified him to teach in primary and secondary schools, his special subjects being rural sciences and gardening. He started his probationary year at a school at Beare Green near Dorking in Surrey in February 1948. Strangely the headmaster, Mr Pyatt, came from Redruth, Bill always spoke of him as a really decent bloke and the best head he ever worked with. During his training the family had remained in Salcombe but now moved to a rented cottage in Holmwood, Surrey. I think his son Tony was born around 1948, but Tony only remembers living in Chagford in mid Devon.

Bill completed his two-year probation in Surrey, but wanted to get back to Devon. Luckily a post was advertised at Chagford on the edge of Dartmoor, and he moved the family back to the westcountry again when he took up the post. A letter welcoming him to the Teign & Dart Association of the NUT gives the date as June 1951.

Chagford at that time was a quiet little town centred on a traditional square. The children came into the school by bus from a large rural farming area which was ideal for Bill's subject. He expanded the curriculum, often taking livestock reared at school to local agricultural shows. Sandra was now at primary school and Tony was a toddler. He remembers 'My earliest memories revolve around Chagford and snow. Our house seemed to face the oncoming wind during heavy bouts of snow and blizzard conditions. Dad would climb out of the bedroom window and down to dig out the front door! When conditions were really bad the children from out of town couldn't get in so the schools would have to close. We would go down the fields with a toboggan; it was always me who went through the ice even though Dad had told me not to! This ended up with me crying all the way home with Dad telling me it was my own bloody fault!

'It seemed that we had the best of both worlds because in the summer holidays we would go to Salcombe on the bus – I was usually travel-sick. To go from the moor to the sea was a marvellous experience for me. I had my own little boat and I would get up before the others and row across the harbour to the beach on the other side of the estuary.

'I was a naughty child and had a few good hidings from Dad which resulted in me telling him that I hated him and would never speak to him again. However 15 minutes later I would be sitting on his lap and he was reading me my *Beano*.'

The mid-50s came and with them another move, this time nearer to his family home in Kingsbridge. Redworth School in

Totnes was advertising a post in charge of rural sciences which suited Bill very well. He soon had the walled garden at the school filled with vegetables and flowers which were sold to the staff and parents. Tony completed his primary years at school and Sandra was finishing her secondary education.

During their time at Totnes, Bill saw more of his brother's four children. They all recall happy times at Bearscombe farm camping and beaching during the holidays. Chris remembers hide-and-seek in the farm woodland with uncle Bill as the hunter, causing great excitement as he pounced on them from hiding. Chris describes himself as the thoughtful one, brother Paul the scaredy one and Tony as wild and fearless. He also remembers Bill as a fun-loving uncle who was full of adventure and who gave them so much to smile about.

Bill joined the Conservative Club and made new friends with whom he spent most winter evenings, enjoying a pint and a game of darts or snooker. The summer months were busy, gardening at the school or fishing off the beach at Salcombe.

The beginning of the new school year, in September 1959, was to bring about changes which took Bill out of his comfort zone and created a whole new life. The customary pre-term staff meeting at Redworth introduced the newly-appointed members of staff, and I was one of those! The headmaster introduced me to Bill and asked him to show me around the grounds as I had to wait an hour before getting a train back to my home in Exeter. Bill was the same handsome man I had noticed across the staff meeting, thinking 'I bet he's married'. Although nothing was said I knew this was going to be special. I left with a huge bunch of beautiful flowers and a feeling that my first teaching post was going to be great.

The school had found me a bed-sit in the main street above a grocer's shop so I was able to walk to school. I soon immersed myself in organising the curriculum for the girls' PE and getting to know the pupils in my registration class. School dinners were eaten in the main hall and the staff had theirs at a table on the stage; that time I spent getting to know the members of staff, especially Bill, who turned out to be a mine of incredible information on anything.

As the '50s turned into the '60s we secretly became a couple of the swinging liberated era. During the two years at Totnes we had both realised the seriousness of our situation and both broke off the affair on different occasions but always found it impossible to keep a distance. In the end fate resolved the situation. I became pregnant which somehow didn't bother me at all, and my instinct was right as Bill began to look for a totally new job away from the westcountry.

One of his farming friends at the club was also a rep for BOCM feed merchants and with his help Bill secured a training place at the company's experimental farm in Stoke Mandeville, Buckinghamshire. He packed a bag, left the family in Totnes and set off for a new life on his Lambretta scooter, riding all the way to Bucks in August 1961. I had left my teaching job at the summer half-term, and following my 22nd birthday, Bill returned to collect me having found a caravan on a pub site for us to live in. He rode his scooter and I followed in my Morris Minor.

The next seven years saw Bill emerging as a poultry farm manager, responsible for thousands of birds from chick to table and we moved four times through four counties! During all this time our four children were born. By 1968 the intensive poultry industry was coming to an end and Bill decided it was time to return to teaching. After several interviews in Cornwall he secured a post at Penryn School, and began teaching in September, living in temporary digs. October came and the Schoolhouse at Halwin was available to rent. We all moved down to Cornwall during half term.

Bill spent the next 20 years at Penryn, developing the gardens to a very high standard which was recognised by the county inspector as a demonstration school garden. He persuaded the council to build an animal house with facilities for pigs, rabbits, poultry, goats and guinea pigs. He joined the school ski-trips each spring half term, learning to ski and visiting Austria, Switzerland, France and Italy several times.

Meanwhile I had returned to teaching, once our four children were all at school. Helston Grammar school had combined with the two existing secondary schools to form one very large comprehensive. They performed regular Gilbert and Sullivan operas, instigated by the head of English, and I joined the group. Eventually Bill also took part and progressed from the chorus to take on varied minor leads.

In 1979 we moved to a smallholding at Wendron where Bill looked after a range of livestock, raising calves and finishing beef cattle which he sold at market. Five years later, in 1984, our two eldest children married their partners in a double wedding. Linda moved to Canada with her husband, a Canadian national, while Michael and his wife set up home in the Helston area.

Bill was beginning to experience problems which seemed to be arthritic so we looked for a property back in the Halwin area. A very run-down bungalow in Penmarth came up for sale and we took on a major renovation project with the help of a local friend who was a great guide and excellent builder.

Two years later a property in Carnkie came on the market with three acres and outline planning for a barn to be converted. On contacting the sellers we discovered they might be interested in buying our bungalow at Penmarth. A satisfactory deal was achieved and we moved in to Mount Joy Farm in the autumn of 1989.

During the first ten years much was changed at the property as many of the concrete outbuildings had to come down in compliance with the barn development plans. Bill stocked the holding with a few yearlings to fatten for market and refurbished the piggery to house a sow. The barn conversion progressed slowly but eventually the smoke rose from the chimney stack for the first time to the cheers of the family.

Bill and I had managed to make several trips to Canada during the '90s to spend time with Linda and her expanding family. Bill loved the huge spaces and beautiful expanses of virgin forest and acres of ranchland. But by now he had been diagnosed with a neural disease which gradually took away all feeling in his feet and hands, progressing slowly to his limbs and body; our younger son Richard now took over the smallholding. Bill had always been very accident-prone but now it became a regular thing because, although in pain, he still battled on regardless. A mobility scooter helped but only when we had a special set of tractor-type tyres fitted which allowed him to get onto the rough driveways and into his garden.

Bill's 80th birthday was celebrated with a family meal at a local hotel, his handsome face now very swollen from the variety of drugs he took. Soon his kidneys began to fail. The new millennium began, the extended family growing ever larger and great-grandchildren increasing in number. Bill was enduring trips to hospital for dialysis three times a week, often returning exhausted or feeling very sick. I was now retired and acting as his fulltime carer, and I persuaded him to write his early memories and wartime experiences, which he managed until he was unable to write or type, whereupon he finally resorted to a tape recorder.

In August 2007, Bill was taken to hospital with a severe case of diverticulitis. He remained there until October when I was told there was nothing more they could do for him; clearly there was an underlying problem, which no-one seemed willing to mention.

Bill desperately wished to return home, but it took some time to arrange for a special bed and other equipment to be installed. Dialysis at the hospital continued for a while, Bill being transferred by stretcher and ambulance, but on his last trip they were unable to continue, and Bill passed away that night with his family at hand.

Over the last two decades, and since Bill's death, there have been many changes in the family, which has become quite extended. Family gatherings are, on the whole, both amicable and raucous. Linda and Richard now own sections of the smallholding, while Michael and Alison are still living nearby.

PICTURE CREDITS

Courtesy of **Kingsbridge Cookworthy Museum**:
4 – 10, 14. Old Kingsbridge.

Courtesy of **Imperial War Museum**:
32. No 1 balloon unit at Cardington (CH17333).
35. Avro-Ansons (C2119).
36. Boulton Paul Defiants (CH884).
40. Wellington bombers of No 214 Squadron at Stradishall (CH3994).
41. 149 Squadron (HU107788).
42. Wellington bomber of 214 Squadron undergoing repairs (CH1415).
44. Short Stirling bombers of 1651 HCU (TR37).
45. Short Stirling (HU107753).
46. pilot and co-pilot (HU107800).
47. bomb-aimer (CH11542).
48. navigator (D4738).
49. Stirling bomber of 1651 HCU (TR8).
50. raid over Hamburg (C3677).
60– 62. Liberated POWs at Fallingbostel (BU 3662, BU 3861, BU 3705).

Courtesy of **Konflikty.pl**:
34. Tiger Moth.

Courtesy of **Fallingbostel Military Museum**:
59. Liberated POWs at Fallingbostel

Other photographs supplied by members of the family.